Grabbing Operas by Their Tales

Liberating the Libretti

Charles E. Lake

Illustrations
Mike Rooth

Sound And Vision

Author's Foreword

There's probably not a better description of what goes on in opera than what Ed Gardner said many years ago, "Opera is when a guy gets stabbed in the back and instead of bleeding, he sings." Without a doubt, singing and music take precedence over realism in an operatic performance. (In fact, some performers insist on singing while the opera is going on.) However, there isn't much mention of singing or music in this book because its focus is on the libretto – the opera text, as it were. It's time for the libretto to be liberated, the tale to be told and the plot to be exposed in some of the best-known and well-loved operas.

Ernest Newman wrote, "Every great opera has a two-fold character; the component parts are supreme music and supreme romance." However, there are other happenings in opera plots besides romance that get our attention. For instance, in the 15 operas in this book, there are 33 violent deaths (including nine suicides but excluding the large, unnumbered body count in the finale of *Samson and Delilah*), 14 occurrences of operatic love at first sight and seven diva dives (where the diva faints or slumps at the end of a scene). Also, there are 14 rather transparent character disguises that somehow fool everyone except the stagehands. (Maybe operas should be labeled MA, for Mature Audiences only.)

Irreverent humor and wordplay have been added to the retelling of the 15 operas for your enjoyment. In addition, a fabricated and unauthorized epilogue has been appended to the end of each opera. It's fun to conjecture what the opera's main characters are doing five years after the opera finale. In some operas this is easy – there aren't many main characters left standing!

Charles Lake
July, 2004

Table of Contents

Opera Wordplay

We've added this set of questions to test your knowledge of some infrequently used words that surfaced in the operas in this book. Do you know the meaning of the words in italics? If you know the meaning of the word, do you know how the word comes to play in the opera? You'll find the meaning of these words and its usage in the opera indicated. Happy hunting!

1. What made Don Jose think about a *plummet*? (*Carmen*, Act I)
2. Why did Siebel put his fingers in a *stoup*? (*Faust*, Act III)
3. What did Faust do on *Walpurgis Night*? (*Faust*, Act V)
4. How did Romeo and his friends use *dominos*?
   (*Romeo and Juliet*, Act I)
5. What was Hansel doing with a *besom*? (*Hansel and Gretel*, Act I)
6. What kind of cookies did the *ogress* like? (*Hansel and Gretel*, Act I)
7. Why did Giovanni give his servant a *Bravo*? (*Don Giovanni*, Act I)
8. How many sets of *dominos* were in Giovanni's garden?
   (*Don Giovanni*, Act I)
9. What did Hoffmann see behind his friend's *portiere*?
   (*Tales of Hoffmann*, Act I)
10. Why did Hoffmann stop the *barcarolle*?
    (*Tales of Hoffmann*, Act II)
11. Where did the painter, Cavaradossi, see the *Sacristan*?
    (*Tosca*, Act I)
12. Why was the crowd in Peking interested in a *Mandarin*?
    (*Turandot*, Act I)
13. How's Don Magnifico's *oneirocritical* talent? (*Cinderella*, Act I)
14. What did Samson do with the *satrap*? (*Samson and Delilah*, Act I)
15. Why did Count di Luna hide his *retainers* in a convent?
    (*Il Trovatore*, Act II)
16. Where was the Pharaoh's *retinue*? (*Aida*, Act II)
17. How did Iago use a *Brindisi*? (*Othello*, Act I)
18. What did Otello get from his *doublet*? (*Othello*, Act IV)
19. How were *thalers* used in *Lohengrin*? (Please don't thay they
    thailed on thips!) (*Lohengrin*, Introduction)
20. What were the knights supposed to do with their *thralls*?
    (*Lohengrin*, Act I)
21. Who wasn't angry, but came and left in a *skiff*? (*Lohengrin*, Act I)
22. What did Siegmund do with the *mead* that Sieglinde gave him?
    (*The Valkyrie*, Act I)

*

Opera Epilogue Conjectures

We've added this set of questions to let you conjecture what some of the opera characters might be doing five years after the opera finale. See if your guess matches ours. You'll find our fabricated and unauthorized epilogue at the end of each opera. There may be a few surprises! Good luck!

1. What happened to Escamillo, the toreador who loved Carmen? (*Carmen*)
2. What happened to Faust? (*Faust*)
3. What happened to the friar who gave Juliet the sleeping potion? (*Romeo and Juliet*)
4. What business is Hansel and Gretel's father in now? (*Hansel and Gretel*)
5. What happened to Leporello, Don Giovanni's servant? (*Don Giovanni*)
6. Did Hoffmann finally have a successful love affair? (*Tales of Hoffmann*)
7. What did Roberti, the designated torturer, attempt in order to change professions? (*Tosca*)
8. What inventions are Ping, Pang, and Pong (the Emperor's Ministers) credited with? (*Turandot*)
9. Did Cinderella's stepsisters get married? (*Cinderella*)
10. Who escaped death when Samson brought down the temple? (*Samson and Delilah*)
11. Under what circumstances does Count di Luna favor capital punishment? (*Il Trovatore*)
12. Were the bodies of Aida and Radames recovered from the tomb? (*Aida*)
13. Did Iago get away with all his lies and deceit? (*Othello*)
14. Did Godfrey recover from his ordeal as a swan? (*Lohengrin*)
15. Why is the goddess Frica so frustrated? (*The Valkyrie*)

**

Dedication

To My Lovely Wife Joyce,
and
To Our Children and Grandchildren
Vicki Lake

Mark and Darlene Lake
Elizabeth, Krystal, and Michael

Bob and Paula Merriman
Bobby and
Hunter

Paul and Linda Lake
Caitlin, Cara, and Cameron
***

Carmen

By Georges Bizet
(1838-1875)
Libretto by Henri Meilhac and Ludovic Halevy
Based upon the story of the same name by the French
novelist Prosper Mérimee

MAIN CHARACTERS

Morales, an Officer of the Dragoons	*Bass*
Micaela, a peasant girl	*Soprano*
Zuniga, a Captain of the Dragoons	*Bass*
Don Jose, a Corporal of the Dragoons	*Tenor*
Carmen, a gypsy girl	*Soprano*
Escamillo, a toreador	*Baritone*
Frasquita, a gypsy friend of Carmen	*Mezzo-soprano*
Mercedes, a gypsy friend of Carmen	*Mezzo-soprano*
El Dancairo, a smuggler	*Baritone*
El Remendado, a smuggler	*Tenor*

Place: In and around Seville, Spain
Time: 1820s
First Performance: Opera-Comique, Paris, March 3, 1875
Original Language: French

Carmen is an opera set in Spain that was composed by a Frenchman, Georges Bizet. It was his most successful work, primarily because he died at the early age of 36, just three months after *Carmen's* premiere. *Carmen* is one of the most reliable box-office successes today, but its Paris premiere in 1875 was coolly received. Maybe the French public and press of that day didn't like women who smoke, gypsies who smuggle, and bullfighters who sing. Whatever. Anyway, *Carmen* is the tragic one-sided love story between a bewitching, sensuous gypsy woman and a hot-tempered army corporal.

ACT ONE

A public square in Seville. On one side of the square is the gate of a tobacco factory. On the other side is a guardhouse. It is noon. Morales and a number of other guards are lolling around their guardhouse. They are approached by a comely girl, Micaela, who says she is looking for a soldier. Morales is quick to volunteer, although volunteering is normally unwise in the army. Micaela hastily refines her request – she wishes to see a specific corporal, one Don Jose. She leaves after the disappointed Morales tells her Don Jose will probably be part of the next changing of the guard. Sure enough, Corporal Jose is one of the new guards who arrive under the command of Captain Zuniga.

The changing of the guard takes place as a group of street urchins marches along with them. Then, as Don Jose exchanges pleasantries with Zuniga, the square fills with young men waiting to ogle the arrival of the girls, especially Carmen, who work in the nearby tobacco factory. (Evidently, Don Jose and Zuniga are working the best shift.) A bell rings from the factory and the girls stream out into the square. The girls are smoking and they compare how lovers' words and promises are like the smoke that ascends to the sky and is gone. (Of course, this is before the Surgeon General's findings on secondhand smoke.)

Then, Carmen makes a dramatic entrance and begins to sing seductively the familiar *Habanera* that expounds her view of love as an emotion that cannot be tamed and must be seized when it happens. The young men are enamored by Carmen, but dutiful Corporal Jose pays her no attention. After Carmen finishes her song, she impulsively takes a flower (probably it's a forget-me-not; unlikely it's a touch-me-not) from her bodice, flings it in the face of Don Jose, and laughingly runs away. A surprised Don Jose feels like a plummet hit him.[1] (Don Jose is probably wondering if this is an example of Corporal punishment.)

He does pick up the flower and smell its perfume. He is perplexed and behaves as if bewitched; thinking that if sorcer esses exist, then Carmen must surely be one. The bell of the factory rings, interrupting his thoughts. The girls return to

---

[1] A plummet is not a bird species; it's really a ball of lead, a bullet.

work and all of the young men leave, since there's no longer any reason to stick around.

Corporal punishment?

Micaela re-enters and greets Don Jose warmly, not realizing a flower has just assaulted the one she loves. She tells Don Jose she has brought some gifts from his mother: a letter, some money, and a kiss. (Some observations: Don Jose evidently has no mailing address, lives beyond his means, and is starved for affection.) Micaela gives him a motherly kiss. In return, Don Jose asks Micaela to tell his mother he loves her. They exchange pleasantries and then Don Jose gives Micaela a filial kiss to deliver to his mother. (Mother and son are quite affectionate with each other when they're not together.) Micaela leaves, envisioning a new career as a courier in the local post office. Don Jose realizes he has been a prodigal son. He plans to correct that soon by marrying Micaela, as his mother wishes.

Suddenly a great uproar is heard in the factory. The girls rush out of the building seeking help. Zuniga and some soldiers go to investigate. They find that two girls have quarreled and one has been hurt. The assailant is Carmen. (This seems more serious than an assault by a flower.) Carmen is taken into custody. She is impertinent and refuses to answer questions. Her hands are bound and she is left in Don Jose's charge while Zuniga, followed by the other soldiers, leaves to write an order for her incarceration.

Alone with Don Jose, Carmen tells him he pleases her and implies they could be lovers. She sings the *Seguidilla* – an invitation for Don Jose to join her at Lillas Pastia's tavern, where they will drink wine and she will dance the seguidilla – which is easier to dance than to say. Poor Don Jose is over-matched – proving Carmen can outsmart Don Jose with both hands tied behind her back. He unties her and she hides her unrestrained hands behind her as Zuniga returns with the written incarceration order. In an aside to Don Jose, Carmen tells him she will push him down on the way to prison and that will allow her to escape. And, that's precisely what happens as the scene ends. Carmen escapes after she gives Don Jose a shove in the back. He's definitely a pushover.

ACT TWO

Lillas Pastia's tavern on the outskirts of Seville. This is the place where Carmen had suggested to Don Jose that lovers come to drink wine and dance. Carmen and two of her gypsy girl friends, Frasquita and Mercedes, are seated at one of the tables in the smoking section of the tavern. Actually, all the tables in the tavern are in the smoking section. Captain Zuniga and some soldiers are seated with Carmen and her friends. (Did we miss something here? Isn't our Captain consorting with a known fugitive from justice?) The place is alive with song and dance. Zuniga has become infatuated with Carmen and asks her to leave with him. (Also, he probably doesn't like all the smoke.) Carmen refuses, which angers Zuniga. He blames her refusal on the fact that he had Don Jose imprisoned for Carmen's escape. Carmen denies his accusation, but is pleased to learn Don Jose was released from prison that day.

As the disgruntled, rejected Zuniga is leaving, voices outside the tavern are heard hailing Escamillo, the victorious bullfighter from Granada. The crowd toasts Escamillo as he enters the tavern. He responds with the famous *Toreador Song* and the crowd joins in on the chorus. While Escamillo is singing, Carmen catches his eye.(Actually both eyes. He remembers that old bullfighter saying, "All work and no play...") When he finishes his aria, he swaggers over to Carmen's table asking for her name so he can invoke it the next time he is in peril. (He doesn't realize the immediate danger he's in – he should talk to Don Jose.) Obviously, the when-I'm-in-peril line is a standard pickup line used by toreadors. Carmen, having been around the bullring a few times herself, is not too impressed, but does give Escamillo her name.

All now leave the tavern except for Carmen and her two gypsy girlfriends. Two known smugglers, El Remendado and El Dancairo, enter the tavern. They plead with the girls to join their next caper. Their argument goes like this ...

"When there's a question of cheating,
by deception or thieving,
to succeed as one ought,
the women must be of the party."[2]

Unable to resist such flattery, Carmen's two girlfriends are ready to help. Carmen, however, tells them she cannot join them because she is in love and waiting for the soldier who helped her escape. At that operatic moment, Don Jose's voice is heard as he approaches the tavern. Carmen's friends tactfully leave, but not before imploring Carmen to enlist Don Jose to be a member of their smuggling ring.

Don Jose and Carmen greet each other eagerly. She begins to dance for him, accompanying herself with castanets. Although Don Jose prefers tambourines, he is highly aroused by watching the sensual Carmen dance. After all, he has been in prison for two months. A bugle is heard in the distance. Don Jose tells Carmen he must return to duty. (He should have

---

[2] No comment.

gotten a three-day pass.) Don Jose's comment angers her, but she continues her dance. The bugle call sounds again, and Don Jose insists he must return to duty. Carmen stops dancing and angrily tells him to scamper back to the barracks. Don Jose tries to tell her of his love and to prove it he shows her the withered remains of the flower she threw at him. He sings the *Flower Song* aria *La fleur que tu m'avais jetee* (See here the flower that once you gave me). He has kept that flower ever since that first day. (Now, where does a soldier keep or wear a flower for two months?) Carmen is not impressed – maybe she doesn't like his "see here" attitude. She tells him if he loves her, he will join her in the mountains and not return to duty. He says he cannot become a deserter and so be dishonored. She says she hates him and she never wants to see him again. Rather than ask for clarification of her comments, Don Jose's clever response is to tell her farewell forever.

A knock is heard at the door, interrupting this warm parting. Captain Zuniga bursts into the room. Zuniga is really a take-charge guy. He chastises Carmen for preferring a mere soldier to an officer. He orders Don Jose to leave. Rank definitely has its privileges. Don Jose refuses to leave, but Zuniga gives him some encouragement by striking him. Don Jose draws his sabre, as does Zuniga. Carmen steps in between the two rivals and calls for help. The smugglers rush in and render Zuniga harmless by pistol point. They tell him he will be taken for a walk until their safety is assured. [3]

Don Jose sees now that he has no choice but to join Carmen and the smugglers. Carmen concludes this scene by singing the song of freedom that describes how pleasant the free and wandering life is. This appears to be a highly debatable point of view.

ACT THREE

A rocky, picturesque and secluded place in the mountains. It is night. The smugglers are resting, making sure the way is

---

[3] A smuggler's walk is not as permanent as a gangster's ride.

clear before they move their goods past the guards at the pass. Carmen is no longer interested in Don Jose. She tells him the gypsy way of life is not for him and he should leave. Don Jose is hopelessly in love with Carmen and warns her she will regret it if she says that again. Carmen says it doesn't matter to her; she will die when fate wills it. She turns her back on Don Jose and goes to sit by her two gypsy girlfriends who are dealing cards to determine who their lovers will be. (Don Jose should join this game: He might learn his love affair with Carmen just isn't in the cards.) Carmen turns some cards to determine her destiny. The cards foretell her death. She reshuffles and turns the cards again – same result – the cards foretell her death. (Carmen should think of playing another version of Solitaire that would be more fun.) She says the cards don't lie, but she is strong and she will defy the fate that the cards are forecasting for her. (In other words, she *discards* the results.)

The smugglers enter and take up their contraband. They decide Carmen and her two girlfriends will entertain the three guards at the pass while the men with their booty sneak by unobserved. (Obviously, they won't shake their booty.) The women quickly agree – they conclude entertaining the guards will be much more fun than just playing cards. The morose Don Jose is told to stay and guard their possessions. They all leave.

Remember, it is night and this place is in a secluded mountain area. Amazingly, Micaela appears, looking for Don Jose. One wonders not only what a pretty girl is doing in a place like this, but how did she find it and how did she get here? [4]

She hides among the rocks when she hears voices. (Hopefully, hearing voices is not a common occurrence.) Escamillo, the singing bullfighter, enters, closely followed by Don Jose. Now everyone has found the hideout of the smugglers except the chief of police. Escamillo tells Don Jose he seeks his new

---

[4] Bizet solved this credibility problem by creating a non-singing role for a Guide, who makes a cameo appearance.

love Carmen. He explains that Carmen is weary of her former lover, an army deserter. Don Jose, being a quick thinker, realizes Escamillo is talking about him. He challenges Escamillo, who now realizes Don Jose is the jilted lover. They draw their knives (when Don Jose was on active duty, he had a sabre) and lunge at each other. Before a killing thrust is made, Carmen arrives and stops Don Jose, as he is about to strike Escamillo. (For all her faults, Carmen seems to be able to stop a good fight – although she normally starts more fights than she stops.) Escamillo, seeing that all the gypsies have returned, decides it's time to head back to the bullring. As he backs away, he generously invites all of them to come to his next bullfight at Seville – supposedly tickets will be at the will-call window. Don Jose is not pleased – the gypsies have to hold him so Escamillo can safely leave.

The gypsies are set to break camp when the hiding Micaela is discovered. All are surprised to see her. (Obviously none of them knew about the Guide.) A three-way conversation takes place between Micaela, Carmen, and Don Jose. Micaela implores Don Jose to return home to his mother. Carmen tells him to leave because the gypsy way of life is not for him. Although he is hopelessly outnumbered, Don Jose insists he will stay because his fate is tied to Carmen. He is adamant he will not give her up to a new lover, much less a civilian. Don Jose's declaration is devastating to Micaela, who loves Don Jose very much. Micaela is forced to play her trump card: She tells Don Jose his mother is dying. Hearing Micaela's bad news changes Don Jose's plans. He realizes he must go see about his mother immediately. He tells Carmen he is discarding her (Don Jose hasn't been listening), but they shall meet again. He leaves hurriedly with Micaela.

ACT FOUR

A square in Seville. However, we're not back at square one – this square is near the arena where the bullfight will take place today. The crowd is moving toward the entrance to the bullring, at the rear of the square. The vendors are selling their wares: oranges, cigarettes, fans, water, wine, and souvenirs. (The bullfight must not be sold out – there aren't any ticket scalpers.) The band of the toreadors heralds the arrival of Escamillo and Carmen as the crowd cheers. Escamillo is magnificently dressed. (One might say he is dressed fit to kill.) He and Carmen tell of their love for each other as Escamillo proceeds into the arena as part of a great procession. Carmen remains outside the arena as her two gypsy girlfriends approach her. Her friends warn Carmen they've seen Don Jose and she should flee. Carmen refuses, saying she is no coward. Cheers are heard from the arena as the bullfight has begun. The square becomes deserted except for Carmen. Everyone else must have tickets.

Don Jose enters and approaches Carmen, begging her to go with him to start a new life together. Carmen tells Don Jose his love for her is in vain and she does not love him. He tells her again how much he adores her. (Don Jose is still not listening.) She tells him again, "I love thee not!" The cheers from the arena interrupt their conversation as the crowd applauds Escamillo's victory in the arena. Carmen is seen to celebrate and she moves toward the arena. Carmen says she loves only Escamillo and throws down a ring that Don Jose had given her. That does it! Don Jose hears the applause for Escamillo and he finally realizes he has lost Carmen. His frustration and jealousy overcome him. He says, "All is ended!" and stabs Carmen, who falls dead. He then cries out, "My beloved Carmen!" and falls across her body as a shocked Escamillo appears from the entrance of the arena.

FIVE YEARS LATER
(A Fabricated and Unauthorized Epilogue)

- Don Jose is serving a life sentence in a prison on the Island of Majorca, where the prisoners make bullfighting souvenirs for sale to tourists.

- Micaela, after a brief stint in a convent, writes an advice-to-the-lovelorn column for the Cordoba newspaper

- Don Jose's mother is quite well, thank you. When Micaela told Don Jose his mother was dying, she was dying, all right – just dying to see her son, that's all. She's in the souvenir business now, with a small souvenir shop by the bullring arena in Seville.

- Escamillo tragically lost his life when he became a casualty in the running of the bulls at Pamplona. It is said that he was singing instead of running.

- Captain Zuniga's whereabouts are unknown. Come to think of it, he hasn't been heard of since the smugglers took him for a walk.

- Lillas Pastia opened a chain of taverns across Spain and retired at an early age.

- Frasquita and Mercedes, the two gypsy girlfriends of Carmen, are card dealers in a casino in the Costa del Sol region.

- El Dancairo and El Remendado, the two smugglers, gave up their life of crime and became government employees.

- The Guide has never been seen again, presumably lost in the mountains.

***

Faust

By Charles Gounod
(1818-1893)
Libretto by Jules Barbier and Michel Carre
Based upon Part One of the poem *Faust* by Goethe

MAIN CHARACTERS

Faust, a scholar	*Tenor*
Marguerite, a young maiden	*Soprano*
Mephistopheles, Satan	*Bass*
Wagner, a young student	*Baritone*
Valentin, a soldier, brother of Marguerite	*Baritone*
Siebel, a youth in love with Marguerite	*Mezzo-soprano*
Martha, a neighbor and companion of Marguerite	*Contralto*

Place: A German village. Time: Sixteenth Century
First Performance: Theatre Lyrique, Paris, March 19, 1859
Original Language: French

For a few years in the 19th century, Charles Gounod was France's leading composer. Much of his success had to do with his collaboration with the librettists Jules Barbier and Michel Carre. They produced several operas together, but none was more successful than their adaptation of Goethe's masterful poem *Faust*. The opera somewhat follows the poem, but maybe not close enough to satisfy hardcore Goethe devotees – traditionally the opera is titled *Margarethe* when staged in Germany. The opera's success was not lost on royalty – *Faust* was the favorite opera of Queen Victoria.

The opera *Faust* is the story of an old, disgruntled philosopher who trades his soul to be young again. Turns out to be a bad trade for all concerned, but that's opera for you.

ACT ONE

As dawn breaks, old Dr. Faust sits alone in his chamber at a table littered with parchments and books. The room is gloomy and old Dr. Faust is even gloomier. In fact, he is very bitter. He complains to himself (no one else will listen) that Nature and his Creator have been unkind to him. He has lived a long life, but in his quest for knowledge, life seemingly has passed him by. (Faust is living proof that there's no relationship between knowledge and intelligence.) He lives sad and solitary. He is ready for death, but death has evaded him. He decides he shall go meet death instead of waiting for death to come to him. He pours poison from a vial into a cup and is ready to drink. As he is about to drink, he hears a chorus of young women outside his chamber singing about love. Dr. Faust listens for a minute, and then he snorts in contempt as he again brings the cup to his lips. Another interruption. This time it's a chorus of plowmen singing on their way to work. Both men and women join together singing their praises and giving thanks to God for such a beautiful day. Faust puts down his cup in disgust. He says God can't help him. God can't give him the love, faith, and youth he wants. He curses his fate and calls on Satan to help him. (Please note – this is not a local call.)

Voila!

Immediately a flash of blinding light occurs and the well-dressed Mephistopheles appears before Faust. (Well, speak of the Devil ...) He says he has come a long way to be there. What can he do for Dr. Faust? Does he want gold? Maybe fame? Perhaps power? Faust tells him there is only one treasure he wants and that is youth (shades of Ponce de Leon). Mephistopheles says Faust's whim is no big deal: He can easily provide Faust his youth for next to nothing. His next to nothing terms are this: "Up here, I am at your service; but down there you will be at mine." (A punster might say Mephistopheles' contract has but one soul purpose.) Not relying on a verbal contract, Mephistopheles whips out a parchment for Faust to sign. Faust doesn't like the terms, especially the "down there" part – to him, that seems like an eternity. Seeing Faust's reluctance, Mephistopheles conjures up a vision of a beautiful young maiden, Marguerite, seated at her spinning wheel. (There's no resemblance in this vision to a portrait of *Whistler's Mother*.) The beautiful vision does it. Faust literally rips the parchment from Mephistopheles' hands and eagerly signs it. Now to seal the deal, Mephistopheles changes the poison in the cup to a potion that he says will give Faust his youth. Faust is more than ready to drink. He toasts the apparition of Marguerite and then drains the contents of the cup. Voila! Instantly the old Faust is transformed into a young, elegant lord. He and Mephistopheles leave together, lustily singing of the pleasures that await a young, handsome man.

ACT TWO

A square near one of the gates of the town. On one side of the square there is a tavern that has a large sign on its roof depicting the god Bacchus astride a wine cask. A spirited fair is in progress. Students, soldiers, townsmen, and young women are strolling about singing of romance and fine wine.

The soldier Valentin enters and joins a group of his friends. Valentin, sad because he is leaving for the war that day, expresses gratitude for the holy medallion his sister Marguerite has given him to protect him in battle. However, he is concerned about leaving her because she will be alone until he returns. Siebel, who loves Marguerite, says he will watch over her, and his other friends say they will also help. Valentin expresses his thanks to his friends and his reliance on God to watch over his sister with the well-known aria *Avant de quitter ces lieux* (Even bravest hearts may swell). He expresses his sadness in leaving his friends, but he looks forward to the glory of battle. Poor Valentin wouldn't report for duty, though, if he knew how little help Marguerite would receive from Siebel and his friends while he is away.

One of their friends, Wagner, a student, wants to change the mood of the group from one of sadness to one of merriment. (Sure, why not? He's not going to war, he's staying at home.) He begins a humorous song about a rat and a cat, but his singing is interrupted by the boisterous entrance of Mephistopheles.

Mephistopheles tells him to continue the song, but Wagner and the students graciously allow the unknown intruder to lead them in a new song. He sings the *Song of the Golden Calf* describing the idolatry of gold and riches. The students merrily but naively join in, not knowing the true nature of their song leader. After they finish, Mephistopheles becomes the life of the party. He examines Wagner's palm and foretells that he will die in battle.[1] Mephistopheles then tells Siebel he is cursed and when he touches a flower it will wilt. (There goes Siebel's career in horticulture.) At this point, the others in the group seem to lose interest in having Mephistopheles predict their future.

Then Mephistopheles drinks to their health, but spits the wine out because he says it is very poor. He looks at the roof of the tavern with the sign showing Bacchus astride a wine cask. He strikes the wine cask on the sign and wine instantly spurts forth from it (hence the saying, "The drinks are on the house!"). He tells the students to drink his good wine as he

---

[1] Hmm — Wagner, the student, must be going to war after all. Something evidently happens to him because we don't see him again after this scene.

proposes an insulting toast to Marguerite. Valentin is greatly disturbed and angered. This stranger has just performed what appears to be black magic and somehow he knows his sister's name. And, he not only knows her name, he is insulting her. He draws his sword and challenges Mephistopheles. Obviously, Valentin has a daredevil attitude.) Wagner and the students draw their swords as well. Mephistopheles draws a circle around himself with his sword. Valentin moves to attack but his sword shatters upon striking the protective circle. Valentin and his friends now realize they are up against a power of darkness and evil. They choose not to attack further. (Swords are expensive and not easily replaced in this part of Germany.) Instead of attacking, they sing the *Chorale of the Swords* and make crosses with their swords, causing Mephis Mephistopheles to cower and back away. The men leave, after which Mephistopheles regains his boldness.

The now young and handsome Faust appears. He is tired of waiting (after all, it's been at least an hour) – he demands to be taken to Marguerite immediately. Mephistopheles tells him to be patient; she will be along shortly. The sound of music is heard (No, no! – not that *Sound of Music*). A group of young men and women enter the square accompanied by several musicians and dance to a lively waltz. Mephistopheles offers one of the girls to Faust, but he is set on wooing Marguerite. Siebel enters and several of the young women want him to dance, but he only has eyes for Marguerite as well. Finally, Marguerite appears and Siebel runs to meet her. However, Mephistopheles blocks Siebel's path and won't let him pass. Siebel backs away – after all, he did see what happened to Valentin's sword. With Siebel out of the way, an unimpeded Faust is able to greet Marguerite. Faust asks her if she will take his arm and walk with him. This pickup line doesn't work: Marguerite shyly refuses.[2] Marguerite leaves without a further

---

[2] Faust is now wondering if he should have used a new line, like, "What's a nice girl like you doing in a place like this?" (In today's world, he might have complimented her by saying, "Nice tattoo!")

word to the disappointed Faust. Mephistopheles laughs at the ineptitude of young Dr. Faust and tells him he needs a lot of assistance with the ladies. They leave together as the young men and women continue dancing.

ACT THREE

Marguerite's garden. At the rear of the garden is a wall with a small door. On one side is a vine-covered bower. On the other, a summerhouse with a window overlooking the flowers and the shrubs. Siebel enters. He picks several flowers, but is dismayed to see that they immediately wilt at his touch, as Mephistopheles had foretold. He decides Mephistopheles' curse can be broken if he dips his fingers in holy water. He goes to the nearby summerhouse, where Marguerite comes to pray. He dips his fingers in a stoup of holy water attached to the wall. His remedy is successful. He picks a small bouquet of flowers (unwilted) and leaves them at the door of the summerhouse for Marguerite. (Siebel is the last of the big spenders – instead of bringing her flowers, he picks them out of *her* own garden.) Unseen by Siebel, Mephistopheles and Faust had entered the garden and watched Siebel pick the flowers and sing of his love for Marguerite. Mephistopheles makes fun of young Siebel to Faust as Siebel leaves.

Mephistopheles leaves Faust briefly while the infatuated Faust sings of his love for Marguerite and how pure and innocent she is. While Faust has been singing, Mephistopheles has been busy. He returns carrying a jewel case for Faust to give to Marguerite. Mephistopheles leaves the jewel case on the steps of the summerhouse where Marguerite will find it. Faust is not sure he should see Marguerite again (If Faust is soul-searching, it's too late – Mephistopheles already has it!). Nevertheless, Faust doesn't stop Mephistopheles from leaving the jewel case by Siebel's flowers. They hide as Marguerite enters. She goes to the bower and seats herself at a spinning wheel. As she spins, she sings the ballad *The King Of Thule* (must be a spinster's tune). She interrupts her singing from time to time musing about the handsome youth who wanted to walk with her.

After she finishes singing, she notices the bouquet by the door and rightly guesses it is from Siebel. (He must have given her her own flowers before.) Then she sees the jewel box. Well, she's pretty sure the jewel box is not from Siebel. She opens the box and is amazed at the many beautiful jewels it contains. She cannot resist trying on all the jewels and looking at herself in a mirror – what woman could have resisted? As she looks in the mirror, she expresses her joy in the aria *The Jewel Song* and imagines she is transformed into a princess.

Martha, a neighbor, enters and compliments her on her looks. The naive Marguerite thinks the jewels were left by mistake, but Martha says the jewels must be a gift to Marguerite from a lord who is in love with her. This is a cue for Faust and Mephistopheles to come forward out of hiding. Mephistopheles wishes to lure Martha away, so Faust and Marguerite may be alone. Good old Mephistopheles tells Martha her husband has died and she should choose a successor. (One has to admit, Meph continues to be the life of the party.) Martha seems to take his news in stride. In an aside, Mephistopheles says that Martha by hook or by crook would probably marry the devil himself. He also says Martha is a bit overripe. Nevertheless, he continues to make advances to Martha until he finally lures her away so Faust can woo Marguerite.

Before he leaves, Mephistopheles instructs the flowers of the garden to intoxicate Marguerite so she will fall in love with Faust. The instructions seem to help. Marguerite picks a daisy and plays "he loves me, he loves me not" with the petals. Naturally, "he loves me" wins. They embrace, but the suddenness of this love makes Marguerite a little faint. After all, she's gone from not holding hands with this stranger to an amorous embrace with him. She tells Faust they must part until tomorrow. She goes into her summerhouse, leaving Faust outside. Faust is about to leave, but Mephistopheles returns, blocking his path. Mephistopheles again razzes Faust about his love-making and tells him the professor needs to go back to school. Mephistopheles tells Faust not to leave yet, but to wait beside the summerhouse for further developments (a Kodak moment?). As they wait outside, Marguerite opens a window and sings of her love for the handsome youth. This is just what the doctor ordered. Faust hastens to her side and they embrace – tomorrow has evidently arrived. Mephistopheles leaves, laughing like ... er, uh ... the devil.

ACT FOUR

(Scene One): Marguerite's room that is rather dark and poorly furnished. She sits at her spinning wheel bemoaning the fact her lover has abandoned her. (Now she is a real spinster.) She still loves Faust, but she does not know where he is or if he will return. She hears the laughter of young women as they pass by her house. She knows they are laughing at her because she is with child and without a lover. As she breaks into tears, Siebel enters and tries to comfort her. He wants to avenge her, but Marguerite seeks comfort only. She still loves Faust. They leave so Marguerite can go to the church to pray on behalf of her unborn child.

(Scene Two): The interior of a church. Marguerite enters, kneels, and begins to pray, but the voice of Mephistopheles is heard calling on evil spirits to dissuade her. (This is probably the first time Meph has been to church in a long time.) Mephistopheles tells her that God has abandoned her and that Hell is waiting for her. Marguerite attempts to continue her prayer for forgiveness. Mephistopheles defies her prayer, saying she is cursed and eternal damnation is in store for her. Marguerite cowers in terror and finally faints.

(Scene Three): A square adjoining Marguerite's house. The war is over! The townspeople are gathered together to welcome their returning heroes. A happy Valentin leads a group of soldiers as they enter the square. The soldiers sing the familiar *Soldier's Chorus* that describes their victory and their bravery in combat. After their joyous singing, all the soldiers gradually leave the square except for Valentin. He sees Siebel among the townspeople and greets him warmly. However, Siebel becomes embarrassed when Valentin asks about his sister. (He should be embarrassed – this is the guy who was going to look after Marguerite, remember?) Siebel's distress arouses Valentin's suspicions and he hurries to Marguerite's house. As Valentin enters her house, Siebel asks him to not be too hard on Marguerite. Siebel leaves – probably correctly thinking it would be best to be out of earshot when Valentin finds out what has happened to his sister while he was gone.

Faust and Mephistopheles enter the square and approach Marguerite's house. Faust still evidently cares for Marguerite, but he will not enter her house. Mephistopheles decides a cruel serenade is in order. He accompanies himself on his guitar while he sings a warning that a girl should not kiss nor open the door until she has a ring on her finger. An obviously insulting song intended for Marguerite (and, an apropos song for young girls today). Valentin rushes from the house and wants to know why they are there and what they want. Mephistopheles answers by saying more or less that it's none of his business. He says the serenade was not meant for him. The angry Valentin realizes the serenade was aimed at his sister and smashes Mephistopheles' guitar with his sword. He wants to know which of the two of them he must strike dead to avenge his sister. (Evidently Valentin doesn't remember the shattered sword incident.) The angry Valentin then throws away the medallion his sister gave him, saying it is cursed. Faust draws his sword as Valentin tells them to be on guard. They begin to fight, but Valentin is fighting a losing battle. Mephistopheles gestures and Valentin's sword is deflected as Faust's sword strikes Valentin a mortal blow.

The fight had drawn spectators, but they kept their distance while the fight was engaged.[3] However, after Valentin falls, many townsmen approach. Mephistopheles quickly takes

---

[3] Some advice from *Poor Richard's Almanac*: "Paintings and fightings are best seen at a distance."

Faust away. Marguerite and Siebel quickly come to the side of the fallen Valentin. Valentin pushes his sister away. He tells her he is dying because of her. Siebel implores Valentin to be forgiving, but Valentin curses her for what she has done. Even the crowd wants him to forgive her, but he tells her that she will die a pauper's death while he dies as a soldier.

ACT FIVE

(Note-Scene One is normally omitted in present day performances.)

(Scene One): A secluded place in the Harz Mountains. Mephistopheles has brought Faust to a part of his kingdom to help Faust cool the fever of his wounded heart. It is a witch's sabbath celebrating Walpurgis Night, when the great beauties of ancient history gather together for a banquet. (Dessert is probably Devil's Food cake.) Faust cares nothing for the festivities: One might say he has a devil-may-care attitude. He is only there to drink and forget. Suddenly a vision of a pale Marguerite appears to him. Faust's drinking to forget plan has obviously failed. He longs to see Marguerite again, because he still cares for her. He insists that Mephistopheles take him to Marguerite at once. So much for Walpurgis Night and so much for meeting some of the great beauties like Helen of Troy and Cleopatra. (Supposedly they hadn't aged.)

(Scene Two): A death cell in the prison, just before dawn. Marguerite is asleep on a pallet of straw in the cell. She is under the sentence of death for murdering her child. Her execution is just a few hours away. She has evidently been driven mad by Mephistopheles' persecution, Faust's abandonment, and Valentin's deathbed curse. Mephistopheles and Faust have gained access and entrance to Marguerite's prison cell (not many people break *into* a prison). Mephistopheles says he will watch outside while Faust helps her escape.

Marguerite awakens from her sleep and embraces Faust although she is obviously confused as to where she is. She begins talking about the day she and Faust first met and fell in love. Faust convinces her to flee with him. She is ready to go anywhere with him until she sees Mephistopheles. She immediately falls to her knees and asks God for forgiveness. Faust frantically begs her to get up and escape with him. His pleas go unanswered. As Marguerite continues to pray, the walls of the prison open and a chorus of angels is heard singing of Christ's glory. Marguerite's plea for forgiveness is answered. Her soul is seen rising up to Heaven. (She appears to be the soul survivor). Faust watches in despair and then he falls to his knees in prayer. Mephistopheles is bent to the ground underneath the sword of an archangel as the final curtain falls.

FIVE YEARS LATER
(A Fabricated and Unauthorized Epilogue)

– Faust is believed to be shoveling coal (you know where).

– Mephistopheles' business is booming. He has been so busy that he found it unnecessary to make any additional public appearances.

– Wagner has become a conscientious objector and flower child. He keeps remembering Mephistopheles predicted that he would die in battle.

– Siebel's career was definitely influenced by wilting flowers. He started his own business, Siebel's Silkies, specializing in silk flowers and lingerie.

– Martha runs weekly ads in the personal section of the local paper. She continues to search for that nice gentleman she met in Marguerite's garden some five years ago.

– The owner of the tavern took down the Bacchus sign over his tavern. Many of his student patrons kept hitting it with their swords in the mistaken idea they would get free wine.

***

Romeo et Juliette
(Romeo and Juliet)
By Charles Gounod
(1818-1893)
Libretto by Jules Barbier and Michel Carre
Based on the tragedy by William Shakespeare

MAIN CHARACTERS

The Capulets	
Lord Capulet	*Bass*
Juliet, Lord Capulet's daughter	*Soprano*
Tybalt, Juliet's cousin	*Bass*
Gregorio	*Baritone*
Gertrude, Juliet's nurse	*Mezzo-soprano*
The Montagues	
Romeo	*Tenor*
Stephano, Romeo's page	*Soprano*
Mercutio	*Baritone*
Benvolio	*Tenor*
And the Others	
Paris	*Baritone*
Friar Lawrence	*Bass*
Duke of Verona	*Bass*

Place: Verona
Time: Fourteenth Century
First Performance: Theatre Lyrique, Paris, April 27, 1867
Original Language: French

Romeo and Juliet has not been as successful as *Faust*, but it is another very successful collaboration of composer Gounod with librettists Barbier and Carre. Many composers were and are inspired by Shakespeare's *Romeo and Juliet,* but Gounod's operatic version is the one that has survived all the others. Gounod's subsequent operas after *Romeo and Juliet* were disappointments. Perhaps he lost his encyclopedia of Shakespeare's works or maybe he couldn't compose operas for performers who didn't have tragic deaths. Whatever the reason, it was downhill for Gounod's operatic career after *Romeo and Juliet*.

The libretto follows the text of Shakespeare's tragedy very closely. The biggest changes are the elimination of several minor characters (guess they couldn't sing) and the addition of Romeo's page (one of those male soprano parts). Oh, yes – in the opera, Juliet manages to wake up before Romeo dies. In that way, they get to sing the closing duet together. A more thoughtful Shakespeare might have ended his tragedy the same way.

PROLOGUE

A short chorus opens the opera and provides the background of the story that follows. Romeo and Juliet fall in love, but they have the misfortune of being from two bitterly rival, feuding families: the Capulets and the Montagues. Normally, family feuds start *after* the marriage.

ACT ONE

A beautifully decorated ballroom in Lord Capulet's palace. A large number of guests are gathered together for a costumed and masked ball celebrating the birthday of Capulet's beautiful daughter, Juliet. As the guests mingle with each other, two close friends enter. Tybalt, a cousin of Juliet, is telling his friend Paris the beautiful Juliet will soon be his bride. Paris replies, "My laggard heart is ready to awake to the mystery of love." Sounds like Paris is really excited. (Does Paris really have a way with words, or is it just wayward words?)

The entrance of Lord Capulet and Juliet interrupts this flowery conversation. Lord Capulet gets the attention of all of his guests and welcomes them to the party. He tells them his heart is filled with pride as he introduces his daughter to his guests. The guests respond by saying how lovely she is. It's one of those social events where everyone is just glad to be there. Waltz music begins. Lord Capulet encourages everyone to dance and enjoy themselves. His guests are happy to oblige;

they all move to the backstage gallery and begin dancing.

Romeo and several other men enter, all wearing dominos.[1] The men are all of the Montague family and they have dared to crash the Capulet party knowing the fracas that will follow if they are discovered. No one else is around or can see them, so they remove their masks temporarily. Romeo is worried. He is concerned they will be recognized and he wants them to leave before there is trouble. He tells his kinsman Mercutio he has a premonition of trouble because of a dream he had the night before. Mercutio laughs at Romeo, saying he is a victim of Queen Mab, the queen of fairies. In his *Ballad of Queen Mab* he tells Romeo that Mab is the queen of illusions; she loves to disturb people's dreams. (Mercutio also believes in Santa Claus, the Easter Bunny and the Tooth Fairy.) Romeo thinks Mercutio is kidding, but he's not sure. However, Romeo is distracted and his fears are quickly forgotten when he spots Juliet among the guests – even at a distance it is love at first sight. (Mercutio is wrong: Queen Mab doesn't own Romeo – Cupid does.) Juliet, however, doesn't notice Romeo or any of the unmasked Montague clan; she is enjoying the party too much. At the moment, Juliet is listening to her nurse, Gertrude, tell her how lucky she is to have Paris as a suitor. Gertrude evidently likes guys with laggard hearts. Juliet pays little attention to Gertrude's comments; her thoughts are on her party and not on suitors or marriage. Juliet expresses her joy in a popular aria known as *The Waltz Song*.

It's time for dinner. (Guests don't dance long at the Capulets' – they like to eat.) The guests leave the ballroom floor and exit to the dining room. The unmasked Romeo makes his move to meet Juliet before she leaves for dinner. He succeeds in intercepting her, and she is alone. They begin with polite conversation, but their words quickly take on a romantic tone. The more they talk, the more they are attracted to each other. Romeo even manages to steal a kiss. (Romeo is a fast

[1] These are not flat rectangular game pieces, but a masquerade costume with a half mask. (Dominos are also worn in one scene in the opera *Don Giovanni*.)

worker.) He begs for more kisses, but their flirtation is interrupted when Tybalt re-enters. It is then Romeo discovers Juliet is a Capulet. Not wanting to start any trouble, Romeo quickly replaces his mask and hastily leaves. It's too late. Tybalt realizes the man who left is Romeo from the hated Montague family. He is outraged that a Montague has the nerve to crash a Capulet party. Even worse, he's sure Romeo was trying to make out with cousin Juliet. (And he's right.) He rushes out to confront Romeo before he leaves the palace. Juliet is greatly distressed. In that brief time with Romeo, she had fallen in love with the handsome stranger (she's a fast worker too). And now she learns she loves a member of the dreadful Montague family. Unhappily she leaves to join the guests.

Romeo, Mercutio and Benvolio re-enter the ballroom on their way out of the palace. An angry Tybalt and Paris are waiting for them. A sword fight appears imminent, but Lord Capulet interrupts their macho posturing. He orders them to cease and desist. (He's heard the local police use that phrase.) He does not want anything to spoil his daughter's birthday party. Tybalt reluctantly obeys his uncle and Paris follows Tybalt's lead. The Montagues quietly leave without further incident. The waltz music begins again. The mini-crisis over, Lord Capulet turns his attention back to his guests. He again encourages them to dance and to enjoy themselves. The evening of merriment continues. (They're having a ball!)

ACT TWO

The Capulet's garden. A balcony, adjoining Juliet's room, overlooks the garden. It is later that evening. Romeo has furtively come to the garden, wanting to continue his courtship of his new love. (Romeo is hoping Juliet isn't leading him down the garden path.) He is not afraid of Tybalt or his threats. He is only afraid that he will not see Juliet again. A light appears in Juliet's window by her balcony and it turns Romeo on. He utters these romantic words:

"But soft, what light through yonder window breaks?
Ah, Love! It is the east and Juliet is the sun!"

Suddenly the sun – er, uh – Juliet appears on the balcony (Romeo is de*lighted* – he always wanted a girl that he could look up to). She confesses her love for Romeo although she did not hear Romeo's words nor is she aware of his presence. Romeo hears her expression of love and is overjoyed. He comes out of the shadows and expresses his love for her. She responds by confessing how much she loves him. They pledge their undying love for each other. (Could this be the start of something serious?) But, their conversation is interrupted when they hear someone coming. They quickly decide they must not be discovered together. Romeo hides back in the shadows of the garden while Juliet leaves the balcony and returns to her chamber.

Romeo always wanted a girl that he could look up to.

Gregorio comes storming into the garden, leading a group of Capulets and Gertrude, Juliet's nurse. They are searching for a page or any of the Montagues who crashed the party. Despite Lord Capulet's wishes for a peaceful night, Gregorio and his men want to punish the Montagues for their insulting behavior. Gertrude tells them she hasn't seen any of the Montagues. She assures them she will tell them if anyone dares to come there. Gregorio's disappointed posse leaves.

Juliet enters the garden. Gertrude scolds Juliet for exposing herself to the night air and, as she enters the house, tells her it's time to retire. As soon as Gertrude leaves, Romeo reappears from his hiding place. He and Juliet continue where they left off. They repeat their love for each other, and now Juliet speaks of marriage. (Yes, despite all the interruptions, this does seem to be serious.) Romeo wants to do more than just talk about marriage – he is ready, willing and able. However, the hour is late and, from within the house, Gertrude calls for Juliet to come inside. (Another interruption.) They realize they must part for now – and they do so with Juliet's familiar words:

"Good night, my love. Parting is such sweet sorrow."

ACT THREE

(Scene One) The cell of Friar Lawrence. It is morning. Romeo enters and greets the good Friar. The Friar is surprised to see him so early in the morning. Romeo tells him he is in love with Juliet. The Friar is somewhat alarmed at the news because he knows the hatred that exists between the two families. Now Juliet arrives. She also tells the Friar how much she loves Romeo. The Friar's fears are dispelled. The two lovers have come to the Friar because they wish to be married immediately. (No doubt – was or is serious.) Their pleas are heeded, and Friar Lawrence agrees to perform the ceremony. (Although it's probably too late to send out invitations.) He hopes their marriage will end the strife between the two feuding families. Gertrude, who came knowingly and approvingly with Juliet, stands watch at the door of the cell while Romeo and Juliet exchange the vows of matrimony. (With Sergeant Gertrude guarding them, they couldn't be safer.) A happy chorus ends the scene.

(Scene Two) A street in Verona by Lord Capulet's palace. Stephano, Romeo's page, is bemoaning the fact that he is unable to locate his master. He wonders if Romeo is still inside Capulet's palace. He strums his guitar and sings a song he knows will provoke the Capulets. When they come out of the palace to challenge him, he will find out where Romeo is. (Did he ever think about just knocking on the door and asking?) His song does its work: Gregorio and several menservants come out of the palace with drawn swords. One insult leads to another and Stephano and Gregorio begin to sword fight. (Stephano is probably thinking now that he should have knocked and asked.)

The fight has just started when two Montagues enter, Mercutio and Benvolio. Mercutio draws his sword and stops the combat. Members of both families back away from each other, but they trade a few more insults and do some serious name-calling. Just as tempers start to settle down, Tybalt enters and tempers flare again. Tybalt challenges Mercutio. But, before they fight, Romeo enters and separates them. This is getting confusing – if there's going to be a fight, who will the combatants be? Tybalt knows who he wants them to be. He has been waiting for this moment. He doesn't care about fighting the other Montagues: He just wants to fight and kill Romeo. He challenges Romeo to fight. The newly married Romeo declines the challenge, not wanting to fight any of his new kinfolk (even if they don't know they're his kinfolk). Tybalt will not take no for an answer, and continues to challenge Romeo. Romeo again declines, saying the time for fighting and such hatred is past. Mercutio decides the Montague honor is at stake, so he accepts the challenge in Romeo's stead. Romeo attempts to prevent the duel, but the fight is on – egged on by other members of the two rival families. The fight does not last long. Mercutio falls, mortally wounded. With his dying words he curses both families (and probably his fencing instructor). Romeo cries out in despair for the loss of his kinsman who died defending the Montague honor. He can no longer be a peacemaker nor can he stay on the sidelines. He seeks vengeance for the loss of his kinsman. Vengeance is his. He engages Tybalt in combat and mortally wounds him.

From his palace, Lord Capulet has heard the disturbance in the nearby street and comes to investigate. He sees the fallen Tybalt and rushes to his nephew's side. As Tybalt lies dying, he asks Lord Capulet to swear that Juliet will marry his good friend Paris. (Well, Lord Capulet's Momma shoulda taught him about swearing – his swearing is gonna cause a few problems.)

The Duke of Verona enters. He is outraged that the peace of Verona has been jeopardized by the hatred that exists between two prominent families. And, now, that hatred has erupted into the death of two people. (And the loss of their tax dollars.) He says the conflict must end immediately. The Capulets could care less about the peace of Verona. They ask the Duke for vengeance – they want Romeo to pay with his life. The Duke, however, determines correctly that Tybalt was to blame for starting the conflict. On that determination, he decides Romeo can live, but he tells Romeo that he is banished from the city forever. (Hmm – forever seems like a long time to Romeo.) The Duke is the final authority of this sentence and punishment. There can be no appeal. (No appeal is correct – the punishment certainly doesn't appeal to Romeo.) Moreover, the Duke tells Romeo the banishment starts immediately: Romeo must leave the city that very night. (Hmm – tonight seems like a short time to Romeo.) Romeo is despondent, thinking he may never see Juliet again and be separated from her forever. He vows he will not allow the banishment to separate them, nor will he allow even death to part them.

ACT FOUR

Juliet's chamber. It is night. A torch lights her chamber. Romeo has made good his promise. Secretly he has made his way to see Juliet at the risk of his life. She tells him she is not angry with him because he killed her cousin Tybalt – Tybalt was Romeo's enemy and she loves Romeo deeply. Her sorrow is caused by their pending separation. They express their love for each other again and again. But, now, daybreak comes and Romeo must leave Verona. They exchange tearful farewells. Romeo leaves as Juliet grieves. (Somehow they overlooked discussing any future plans.)

It's only daybreak and some other people in Verona are early risers. Gertrude enters and tells Juliet her father is coming. She tells Juliet he still doesn't know about her marriage to Romeo. Lord Capulet and Friar Lawrence enter. Lord Capulet is surprised Juliet is up early, but he supposes it's because she is mourning her cousin's death. Lord Capulet is wrong. He tries to comfort her by giving her a nice surprise. He tells her that he is going to fulfill Tybalt's dying wish – Juliet is to be married that very day to Paris. It's a surprise to Juliet all right; she almost faints. (Two weddings to two different grooms in two days are probably too much for any bride.) Gertrude and Friar Lawrence tell her to be calm. Juliet decides it's not time to tell her father about her nice surprise. She tries to look pleased and she manages to stay calm until her father and Gertrude leave. Then she asks the Friar for his help. She has been silent and kept her marriage secret as the Friar recommended – now she says that she has no choice but to die. Friar Lawrence tells her to remain calm; he has a solution.[2] He offers Juliet a potion that will cause her to fall asleep and make her appear to be dead. (Cynics of this story might ask why the good Friar carries this potion around with him.) The Friar tells her that after she drinks the offered potion, no one will be able to tell she is still alive. (We've all had blind dates like this.) She will appear to be dead, but she will just be in a deep, death-like sleep. Then, tomorrow she will awaken from her sleep and she can go away with her husband and lover, Romeo. No one will know or suspect what is happening. He asks if she is afraid. Juliet is not. She asks no questions – she takes the flask containing the potion from the Friar and quickly drains its contents. The good Friar leaves.

Lord Capulet and his entourage return to escort Juliet to be married. Juliet starts to leave with them but the quick-acting potion begins to take effect. She falls as if dead. Lord Capulet and his household cry out in horror as they rush to her aid. They are unable to revive her.

---

[2] Is this a play on words? Is the good Friar talking about the solution being an answer to Juliet's problem or is the solution merely a mixture of some kind? Stay tuned.

ACT FIVE

The Capulets' burial vault. (Like all burial vaults, it's basically unfurnished.) Juliet lies on a bier, apparently dead. (Some advice: Never, ever lie down in a burial vault or a funeral parlor.)

Romeo enters and expresses how beautiful she looks even in death. He's inconsolable because he believes she is dead. Romeo has not been told nor notified about the hoax being perpetrated on the Capulet family and Paris. Romeo should have received a letter from Friar Lawrence explaining that Juliet was only sleeping, but Romeo never received the letter. (Insufficient postage or just a bad zip code?[3]) Romeo laments her death, but says death cannot part them; he will join her. He drinks from a small flask containing poison. Juliet awakes, startling Romeo. (Come to think of it – that would be quite a startle.) They tell of their love for each other and embrace. They sing *Viens, fuyons au bout du monde* (Come, let us fly to the ends of the Earth). Unfortunately, they're not going to fly anywhere. (They won't even get to the runway to taxi.) The poison Romeo drank begins to take effect. He staggers and almost falls. He tells the bewildered Juliet he drank the poison thinking she was dead. Juliet cries aloud; she says she cannot live apart from him. Alas, there's no poison left in Romeo's flask. Desperately, she seizes Romeo's dagger and stabs herself. (Both of them will probably never forgive Friar Lawrence.) They embrace and die in each other's arms. (The crime scene investigator will probably never be able to figure this one out.)

---

[3] Actually, Friar Lawrence had dispatched Romeo's page to deliver the letter, but the page was attacked and wounded to the extent that he could not deliver it to Romeo. All this is normally explained to the audience in the prelude to Act Five. Our apologies to the Verona post office, if they are offended.

FIVE YEARS LATER
(A Fabricated and Unauthorized Epilogue)

– Lord Capulet honors Juliet every year by giving a charity ball in her honor. (He needs the money.)

– The Duke of Verona has tired of collecting swords and other paraphernalia of people he banished. He's planning a gigantic palace sale this year. (He needs the money also.)

– Gregorio and Benvolio were both slightly wounded when they fought in a sword duel. Both were banished by the Duke of Verona. Their whereabouts are unknown.

– Gertrude, Juliet's nurse, had her license revoked because of Juliet's death. She now works for a Verona funeral home (without patients).

– Stephano, Romeo's page, left employment of the Montagues. He works as an usher downtown in the Arena di Verona.

– Paris, the rejected suitor and would-be bridegroom of Juliet, is still unmarried. Evidently he still possesses a laggard heart.

– Friar Lawrence never told anyone the truth about Juliet's feigned death. He renounced his calling and moved to Venice. He is now a pharmacist.

– The Verona medical examiner could never agree with the crime scene investigator as to the causes of the deaths of Romeo and Juliet. The Verona police have officially closed the case as unsolved.

***

Hansel und Gretel

(Hansel and Gretel)
By Engelbert Humperdinck
(1854-1921)
Libretto by Adelheid Wette (the composer's sister)
Based upon the fairy tale of the same name by
Jacob Ludwig Carl & Wilhelm Carl Grimm

MAIN CHARACTERS

Hansel, a young boy	*Mezzo-soprano*
Gretel, Hansel's young sister	*Soprano*
The Witch	*Mezzo-soprano*
Gertrude, mother of Hansel and Gretel	*Soprano*
Peter, their father, a broom-maker	*Baritone*
The Sandman	*Soprano*
The Dew Fairy	*Soprano*

Place: In a forest near the Harz Mountains
Time: Medieval
First Performance: Hoftheater, Weimar; December 23, 1893
Original Language: German

Hansel and Gretel was composed and written by a real brother-sister combination about a fictional brother-sister. The real brother, Engelbert Humperdinck, was the composer and his sister, Adelheid Wette, was the librettist. (Would it be inappropriate to ask if the libretto is all Wette?) Engelbert, a disciple of Richard Wagner, is remembered for this opera, not for any of the other five he wrote.[1] Perhaps his name was too long for programs and theatre marquees. Sister Adelheid Wette, who probably married to shorten her last name (al- though it didn't seem to help her career), adapted the libretto from the familiar fairy tale by Grimm.

---

[1]One of his five operas is *Konigskinder*. That one also had a witch and a broom-maker, but the main characters in it don't fare so well. Well, as a matter of fact, they die.

Adelheid should be given credit for getting this opera started. She had her brother to set to music four folksongs from the Grimm fairy tale for a private performance by her children. The performance went so well that Engelbert decided to make a full-fledged opera from it. The rest, as they say, is history.

Of interest in this opera are the main characters in the cast. They're all basically sopranos except one. The token baritone part was probably dictated by some equal-opportunity government requirement. Surely some allowance could have been made for something other than a soprano in the role of the Sand*man*. Give us a break.

ACT ONE

A broom-maker's poorly furnished hut (no computer, no DVD, no VCR, no microwave oven, not even a TV). In the background are a door and a window looking out into the forest. Hanging on the walls are a number of brooms of various sizes and shapes. The broom-maker's children are busy at work. Gretel is seated by the fireplace, knitting a stocking. Hansel is sitting by the door, making a besom (a besom is a poor man's broom, normally made of twigs).

Hansel is hungry; he complains he has had only hard bread to eat for weeks. Gretel sympathizes, but tells her brother to be patient. She tells him their mother has been given some milk by a neighbor and they're due for a rice-blancmange after she comes home. Hansel is delighted thinking about some food coming his way. (He thinks he's getting his just desserts.) He's so excited that he stops working, which influences Gretel to stop working also. She decides to dance and encourages Hansel to dance with her. She teaches him a song and dance that either their grandmother taught her or she saw in some old Danny Kaye movie:

"With your foot, you tap, tap, tap.
With your hands, you clap, clap, clap.[2]

[2] Don't try this at home if your electrical equipment is hooked up to a "Clapper".

Right foot, first. Left foot, then.
'Round about and back again!"

They dance and dance and dance. Faster and faster they twirl until finally they lose their balance and fall to the floor laughing.

As luck would have it with unlucky, unruly children, their mother, Gertrude, arrives home early. The children jump up and attempt to offer their excuses – each sibling attempts to blame the other. However, their mother interrupts them (she is familiar with their finger-pointing). She gives them both a good tongue lashing about their playing while their parents are slaving away. She has lost faith and patience with her children's work ethics. She's got definite ideas as to what the children should be doing. In her mind, Gretel needs to tend to her knitting. And, Hansel? Why, he ought to be making a bundle. No doubt when her broom-maker husband comes home, she will have him make some sweeping changes.

But now, in her anger, she knocks over the jug containing the designated dessert milk. The jug breaks, spilling all the milk – oh, oh! There goes supper. Mother is really upset now, but she's not going to cry over spilt milk. She chases the children out of the house and into the forest. She warns them to return only after they pick enough wild strawberries to fill a basket she has given them. Her anger subsiding, she falls exhausted in a chair and worries how to feed her starving family. (Strawberries can only go so far.) She falls asleep.

A cheery voice is heard singing in the distance. It's the father, who enters the hut in a jovial mood. Peter evidently had an unusually good day at the market selling his wares and maybe a better time at the tavern on the way home. He wakes his wife to tell her the good news (about sales at the market, not ales at the tavern). He shows her all the food he's brought home and she is ecstatic. When he asks about the children, she is not ecstatic. She tells him about their indolent behavior and the breaking of the milk jug. But, now that they have plenty of food, they not only don't cry over spilt milk, they even laugh about it.

Then Gertrude tells him she sent the kids into the forest to get some strawberries. When Peter hears the children have gone into the forest this late in the day he becomes alarmed. He tells Gertrude about the stories of an ogress who lives in the woods near Ilsenstein (which is not to be confused with Einstein, Frankenstein, or even a beer stein).[3] The stories describe how she lures young children with sweets, pops them into an oven and turns them into gingerbread children for eating. Gertrude is horrified. All of us are. After all, the story of a witch who turns children into gingerbread for eating is not in good taste. (In fact, the story is extremely distasteful.) Peter and Gertrude are frightened. Together they run from their hut (and these wordplays) to find their children.

ACT TWO

It is sunset in a clearing in the middle of the forest. In the background is the Ilsenstein. On one side is a large tree, under which Gretel is sitting while she makes a garland of flowers. She is singing a delightful German folk tune, *Ein Mannlein steht im Walde* that likens a mushroom to a man (a one-legged man, no doubt). There are some bushes nearby where Hansel is looking for strawberries.

Hansel can't keep his mind on work. He definitely is not an "all work, no play" guy. He playfully puts Gretel's garland on her head and pays her homage by kneeling before her and giving her some strawberries. She returns the favor. One thing leads to another and the children begin to argue over the strawberries. Finally, Hansel wrestles the basket away from her and eats all the strawberries. Now they've done it – no strawberries and it's too dark to find some. They can't go home empty-handed. And, now, it's so dark they've lost the path that leads them home. They have no choice but to spend the night where they are. They are scared and cling to each other as they hear the night noises of the forest. It doesn't help when

[3] An ogress is a female. All these years you've heard about ogres and you probably never knew that an ogre has always been a guy – a bad guy at that.

they see the figure of a *man* approaching them as complete darkness comes upon them.[4]

The Sandman strewing his sand

The *man* speaks to them gently and the children gradually calm down. The *man* is the Sand*man* who strews sand in their eyes (and looking around in the audience, it looks like *he* strewed some sand their way also). The children are half-asleep, but they remember to say their prayers. They kneel to sing the well-known *Children's Prayer*, asking for guardian angels to watch over them. They fall asleep.

While they sleep, the children's prayers are answered. A bright light shines through the darkness revealing a staircase leading down to the feet of the children. Fourteen angels descend slowly down the staircase and surround the children as guardians. (These 14 are probably all sopranos, also – what's your guess?)

[4] In this scene, there's a lot of singing back and forth between the children, a Cuckoo, and an Echo. Because this dialogue doesn't add to the plot one way or another, both interested readers are directed to the libretto.

ACT THREE

It is morning. The angels have gone. A Dew Fairy approaches the sleeping children and shakes dewdrops on them as she sings softly. She leaves as the children awaken. The children compare notes about a "dream" each of them had. They realize the dream must have been real – the angels were really there! The children are not afraid now. In the morning light the forest is not the scary place it was in the darkness of the night before. The last of the morning mist disappears and they see a charming little house nearby. They decide to investigate further; perhaps they can get something to eat. They make their way toward it; not realizing this is the place their father was warning their mother about.

The children arrive at the house and stare at it in astonishment. A house made of chocolate cream, sugar, raisins, and other goodies stands before them. (*Home Sweet Home* comes to mind – it's certainly not a crummy house.) Near the house on one side is a large oven. On the opposite side there is a cage. All around the outside of the house are some gingerbread figures holding hands and forming a hedge. The children tiptoe cautiously closer to the house. Finally, courageously, Hansel breaks off a bit of cake from a corner of the house. He eats it and tells Gretel how good it tastes.

A voice inside the house asks who is nibbling on her house. The children say it is the wind, while they help themselves to some larger portions of the siding. Again, the voice inside asks who is nibbling. Again, the children respond it is the wind. (Evidently the children do not realize the wind doesn't talk.) The children are having their cake (and eating it too) when suddenly a door of the house opens and a witch, inaccurately and indelicately named Rosina Dainty-Mouth, comes out, confronting the children. She cackles as she throws a rope around Hansel. He manages to get loose and attempts to run away with Gretel. The Witch is too quick for them. She takes a juniper bough from her girdle (nice holster) and does a hocus pocus or two (what is the plural of hocus pocus?) that enchants the children and stops them in their tracks.

She locks up the somewhat paralyzed Hansel in a cage. She takes up the juniper bough again and disenchants Gretel (would her magic words be pocus hocus or sucoh sucop?). She tells Gretel to set the table or she will lock her up, too. Gretel does as she was told. Hansel pretends to be asleep. The Witch sings loudly and happily about fattening up Hansel before he is put on her menu. In the meantime, she heats up her large oven in preparation of baking Gretel for her next meal – ladies first!

The Witch is beside herself (what bad company!) with glee thinking of her upcoming dinner – after all, she has no microwave and there are no fast-food places nearby. In her happy mood, she takes what might be called a flier. She grabs a broomstick and begins to ride around the room on it. (These are not normal broomsticks – they're made only for travelling and have a three-year warranty.) She sings excitedly while she is riding. Speechless (or maybe just song less), Gretel watches from the window.

After the Witch's wild ride and her excited singing is over, she dismounts and goes to wake Hansel. Licking her chops, she asks to see his thumb – Hansel alertly pokes out a small stick for her to feel instead of his thumb. She is fooled into thinking Hansel is scrawny. (Witches are known to have poor eyesight, as well as bad breath.) She calls for Gretel to bring food for Hansel to eat. Gretel brings the food and the Witch begins to force-feed Hansel.

While the Witch is occupied with Hansel, Gretel sneaks behind her, takes up the juniper bough, aims it at Hansel, and repeats the magic disenchantment words. The disenchantment works and the Witch is unaware Hansel is no longer enchanted. (One might say both of the children have become disenchanted with the Witch's magic.)

Convinced all is well, the Witch goes to the oven, opens it, and asks Gretel to peer into it to see if the gingerbread is ready. Gretel acts like she does not understand – a real babe in the woods. The Witch insists Gretel peer into the oven, but Gretel continues to play dumb. She asks the Witch to show her how. In the meantime, Hansel escapes from the cage. The Witch becomes impatient – she decides she will show Gretel what she wants her to do. She opens the oven door and peers into the oven. The children take advantage of their opportunity. Both Hansel and Gretel rush forward, push Rosina Dainty-Mouth into the oven, and slam the door.

Hansel and Gretel are relieved and overjoyed; they sing the *Knusperwalzer* (The Crust Waltz) as they celebrate their victory. They begin eating the sweetmeats of the house. (They are absolutely eating the late Witch out of house and home.) Meanwhile the oven grows hotter and hotter until it finally bursts. To their astonishment, the gingerbread figures that surrounded the house are suddenly transformed into the children they were before they fell under the spell of the Witch. Their eyes are closed, but when Gretel touches them, their eyes open although they remain motionless. Gretel solves that problem with the Witch's trusty juniper bough and the magic disenchantment words. The Witch's spell is broken. The gingerbread children come back to life.

To complete this happy ending, Father and Mother rush in and joyfully embrace their children (although a person from Child Protective Services is seen lurking nearby). The baked gingerbread witch is brought from the ruins of the oven to the middle of the stage and all join in on the closing, grateful chorus:

"When past bearing is our grief,
Then God, the Lord, will send relief!"

Author's note: After seeing this opera, many people have decided they will never eat gingerbread again. I know I won't. Editor's note: Me neither.

TWENTY YEARS LATER [5]
(A Fabricated and Unauthorized Epilogue)

– Peter, the father, sold his broom business and now has the regional franchise that sells and maintains vacuum cleaners. He is cleaning up.

– Gertrude, the mother, does community service work with wayward children. She served briefly as a guard at one of the state prisons.

– Hansel worked for his father a few years, but he didn't like steady employment. He now has jobs that require him working for only a few months a year. Primarily he sells Christmas trees out of the local forest. He also sells sunglasses whenever there is an eclipse of the sun.

– Gretel married a magician and tours with him internationally. She still has the witch's juniper bough, but it's not part of their act. It seems like there's no magic in it anymore. (Maybe it needs new batteries.)

– The Sand*man* retired ten years ago because of back problems resulting from carrying heavy sandbags. After *he* stopped carrying the sandbags, *his* voice changed from soprano to bass.

– The Dew Fairy is unemployed due to weather conditions beyond her control. She doesn't do dew anymore.

– The Witch has been preserved in her gingerbread form. She and her broom are on display in the national museum. The museum sells gingerbread cookies and other souvenirs in her image. They are well done.

– The Gingerbread Kids returned to their homes and grew up like normal children their age. They do have recurring bad dreams about being part of a fence. They meet annually on the anniversary of the witch's death to hold hands and repeat 10 times in unison, "We are not a fence. We are not a fence." It hasn't stopped their bad dreams.

[5] Nothing had changed much after only five years, so this epilogue is 20 years later.

Don Giovanni

By Wolfgang Amadeus Mozart
(1756-1791)
Libretto by Lorenzo da Ponte

MAIN CHARACTERS

Don Giovanni, a licentious young nobleman	*Baritone* or *Bass*
Don Pedro, Commandant of Seville	*Bass*
Donna Anna, the Commandant's daughter	*Soprano*
Don Ottavio, Donna Anna's fiancé	*Tenor*
Donna Elvira, a noble lady	*Soprano*
Leporello, servant of Don Giovanni	*Bass*
Zerlina, a peasant girl	*Soprano*
Masetto, a peasant, Zerlina's fiancé	*Bass* or *Baritone*

Place: In and around Seville, Spain
Time: The Seventeenth Century
First Performance: Natural Theatre, Prague; October 29, 1787
Original Language: Italian

Don Giovanni (or in Spanish, *Don Juan*) is one of three great operas that resulted from the collaboration between the composer Mozart and the librettist Lorenzo da Ponte (the other two operas are *Le Nozze di Figaro* and *Così Fan Tutte*). Mozart classified his *Don Giovanni* as light opera, but there are many opera aficionados who consider it to be a trifle more serious, considering what happens to Don G in the last act. Regardless of the classification, it certainly is one of Mozart's finest operas.

Don Giovanni is the story of the legendary Spanish seducer whose lust for the ladies and his indecent, unseemly conduct gets his just desserts in the end. One might say he made his bed – let him lie in it.

ACT ONE

(Scene One): A courtyard adjoining the Commandant's Palace in Seville. Leporello, a servant of the nobleman Don Giovanni is seated near the entrance to the palace. It is night and only the moon illuminates the scene. Leporello is depressed because he is overworked and underpaid (join the rest of us). Here he is at midnight keeping watch while his master is probably making love to another woman. And not just any woman, she is Donna Anna, the Commandant's daughter, who is betrothed to another. Hearing a loud commotion, he hides. His master, Giovanni, and Donna Anna rush in. Donna Anna is angry and struggling violently with Giovanni. Evidently Giovanni had secretly entered her apartment and made advances toward her under the guise of her be-trothed, Don Ottavio. When she discovers he is not Ottavio, she screams for help and tries to unmask the intruder. The conditioned Leporello, in an aside, says, "Master's in another mess."

Master's in another mess.

Donna Anna's father, the aged and decrepit Commandant, hurries into the room with a torch in one hand and a sword in the other. Donna Anna leaves to get additional help. The

Commandant attacks Giovanni, who knocks the torch from his hand (to engage in Don Giovanni's pastimes, one has to be a lover *and* a fighter). He easily parries the old man's thrusts and finally mortally wounds him. (This is one old soldier who doesn't just fade away.) Giovanni leaves hurriedly. The faithful but scared Leporello follows. Donna Anna returns with her betrothed, Ottavio, and several servants, who discover the lifeless body of the Commandant. Donna Anna is distraught. She vows to dedicate her life to finding and punishing her father's killer. Ottavio, occupying the betrothed position, is required to likewise vow.

(Scene Two): A desolate country road outside the city walls. There is an inn nearby. It is early morning. Giovanni and Leporello are engaged in deep conversation. Giovanni is already thinking of his next conquest while Leporello bewails Giovanni's manner of living. Leporello is quieted when Giovanni threatens him. A veiled woman enters, crying revenge against one who loved her several years ago and then abandoned her. Giovanni says he wants to console her. Leporello volunteers another aside, "Sure! Just like he has consoled fully 1,800 others!" Oh, oh! When Giovanni approaches her, he discovers the veiled woman is a former girl- friend named Elvira. And he is the guilty party Elvira is angrily complaining about. He tells her he had good reason to leave her and his servant will give her an explanation. With that, Giovanni beats what is technically called a hasty retreat.

Leporello is left with the task of calming one of his master's old girlfriends. He takes a book from his pocket and sings the famous *Catalogue Aria* describing and enumerating Giovanni's conquests: 640 in Italy, 231 in Germany, 100 in France, 91 in Turkey and 1,003 in Spain. (These are unaudited results.) There were country girls, city girls, young ones, old ones, fat ones, thin ones, rich ones and poor ones. He concludes his aria by telling Elvira if it's a woman, then Giovanni feels obliged to conquer her, just like he did you. (Nice going, Leporello – that will calm her.) Elvira is infuriated. Her craving for revenge is increased twofold.

Don Giovanni

(Scene Three): A village on the outskirts of Seville near Giovanni's castle. It is the next day. The villagers are singing and dancing in celebration of the upcoming wedding of Zerlina and Masetto, two of their peasant colleagues. Giovanni and Leporello enter, and Giovanni immediately spots the attractive Zerlina. Feigning friendship, he tells Leporello to take the whole party to his castle and entertain them. Especially he wants Leporello to keep Masetto occupied, as he will bring Zerlina along later. Masetto objects, but when Giovanni makes a threatening gesture to his sword, Masetto reluctantly leaves with all the others. (Masetto, unlike Giovanni, is only a lover.) As soon as Giovanni and Zerlina are alone, Giovanni tells of his love for her – even promising to make her his wife. What a line. (He doesn't mean his wife – he means a statistic.) Zerlina is overwhelmed and begins to succumb to this smooth-talking cavalier. Just as they are about to leave together, Elvira enters – she has overheard the conversation and she rescues Zerlina from Giovanni's clutches. The women leave as Giovanni curses his bad luck.

Then Donna Anna and Ottavio arrive. Ottavio greets Giovanni warmly, alleviating Giovanni's fears that he had been recognized as the intruder who killed Donna Anna's father. On the contrary, they recruit Giovanni to help them find the culprit. Elvira re-enters. She accuses Giovanni of betrayals, lies and misdeeds. Giovanni tells the others Elvira is demented. Elvira pleads with them to not believe nor trust Giovanni. Giovanni insists Elvira is mad. Separately and angrily they leave.

Donna Anna and Ottavio have listened, but said nothing while Giovanni and Elvira were trading accusations. Now, after the two accusers leave, Donna Anna has second thoughts. She tells a surprised Ottavio that she recognizes Giovanni's voice and he is the culprit who killed her father. Ottavio expresses his disbelief that Giovanni could be the murderer. Donna Anna is positive, however. She calls on Ottavio to renew his vow for vengeance. After she leaves, Ottavio sings of his astonishment that a friend could do what Giovanni has done. He vows he will get at the truth for the sake of his love.

(Scene Four): The garden of Giovanni's castle. It is later that afternoon. Leporello is explaining to Giovanni what a great job he has done for his master by entertaining the guests and relieving Masetto of his jealousy. Giovanni gives him a few Bravos.[1] Leporello also describes how Elvira and Zerlina came to the party where Elvira said all manner of bad things about Giovanni. Leporello waited until she was finished and then he escorted her outside and locked her out. Leporello gets an extra Bravo for this one. Giovanni changes the subject. He tells Leporello these peasant girls are to his liking and he wants to have a magnificent party without delay. They enter the castle to begin preparations for the party.

Zerlina enters the garden with a disconsolate and cross Masetto. She pulls out all stops, convincing him that he has nothing to be jealous about. He caves in, saying, "O, a man is the weakest thing in Nature." (Especially when a woman is involved.) Masetto acts like he is leaving, but he hides in the garden as he sees Giovanni coming. Masetto wants to see if Zerlina is really faithful. Giovanni enters and sees Zerlina seemingly all by herself. He wastes no time in again trying to lead Zerlina astray. He doesn't get very far this time because Masetto quickly confronts him. (Masetto seems to have gained some courage.) Giovanni adjusts adroitly to the surprise of Masetto's confrontation. He tells Masetto he should not abandon his pretty fiancée and he gallantly leads them both inside to join the party.

Donna Anna and Elvira enter the garden, escorted by Ottavio. All are wearing dominos.[2] They came in costume in order to crash Giovanni's party. They are not recognized by either Giovanni or Leporello and so are invited inside the castle. Before they enter the castle, they temporarily remove

[1] A Bravo is an Italian "Atta boy!" – given in lieu of compensation.
[2] These are not flat rectangular game pieces, but a masquerade costume with a half mask. (Dominos are also worn in one scene in the opera *Romeo et Juliette*.)

their masks and sing the beautiful *Mask Trio*, a petition to heaven for vengeance.

(Scene Five): The party is taking place in a magnificent suite of apartments in Giovanni's castle. The apartments are beautifully decorated and illuminated with candelabra. There are several bands of musicians playing and many revelers who are drinking and dancing in each of the apartments.

The three masked avengers, Ottavio, Donna Anna, and Elvira have entered and have mingled with the revelers without being noticed. The three avengers are closely watching Giovanni's every move. Giovanni is dancing with Zerlina in front of the jealous Masetto. Leporello, the obedient servant, occupies Masetto by forcing him to dance with him. (Doesn't Masetto have any pride?) Thus, while Masetto is distracted, Giovanni steers Zerlina out a side door. (Evidently Giovanni believes the third time is a charm.) Leporello follows. Suddenly screams are heard from the other side of the door. Zerlina rushes back seeking help, followed closely by Giovanni and Leporello. (Giovanni has just learned the third time isn't a charm.) The three avengers remove their masks and confront Giovanni. Giovanni attempts to place the blame on his poor frightened and bewildered servant, Leporello. Leporello is obviously cowed by Giovanni (and obviously underpaid, like he was insisting earlier in Act One). The avenging trio isn't fooled by Giovanni's ploy. Ottavio approaches Giovanni with a drawn sword. Giovanni laughs at all of them (rather a cavalier attitude) and he beats another hasty retreat, this time from his own castle.

ACT TWO

(Scene One): An open plaza in Seville. Nearby is a house with projecting windows on the upper floor where Elvira has taken up residence. Another day has passed; it is early in the evening.

Giovanni enters followed by Leporello. Leporello is telling Giovanni he is quitting because Giovanni sought to kill him (picky, picky). Giovanni said it was all a joke and gives him a purse of money for his trouble. Leporello decides he has a good sense of humor and gladly accepts the gratuity. Giovanni has another job for him, but Leporello wants him to agree to give up women. Giovanni says women are necessary for him more than the air he breathes. Also, he says that to be faithful to one would be unkind to all the others. Modesty is not Giovanni's strong point.

Giovanni has no intention of negotiating further with Leporello now that he has paid him off – he tells Leporello to exchange his cloak and hat with him pronto. Giovanni wishes to court Elvira's pretty maid and believes he will have better luck if he dresses and disguises himself as a servant. They make the exchange.

Then, Elvira appears by an open upper story window that overlooks the plaza. She fears her heart still belongs to the deceitful Giovanni. Giovanni decides to take advantage of the situation. He stands behind Leporello, who is now dressed like Giovanni, and implores Elvira to forgive him and come to him. Elvira cannot resist the sweet-talking Giovanni and comes downstairs. He then tells Leporello to continue the sham by embracing her and then taking her off somewhere to make love to her. Of course, this ruse will allow Giovanni to have free access to Elvira's pretty maid. The hoax works. Elvira thinks Leporello is Giovanni and greets him more than warmly.[3] As they are getting even further acquainted, the real Giovanni leaps out in front of. them and pretends to be a robber assaulting them. They flee as Giovanni laughs about this bit of chicanery.

The stage is now set for Giovanni to court Elvira's pretty maid without any interference. He whips out his mandolin and begins to serenade her with one of the best-known numbers of the opera, *Deh vieni alla finestra* (Come to the window). A beautiful serenade, but terrible timing. Here comes an angry Masetto and a group of armed peasants looking for Giovanni. They think they are talking to Leporello. Giovanni,

---

[3] Elvira says she's all aflame for him. Leporello, disguised as Giovanni, says that he is all ashes.

feigning helpfulness, sends Masetto's posse off in all directions, leaving him alone with Masetto. Masetto tells him he is intent on killing Giovanni and shows him the musket and pistol he has. Masetto is no match for Giovanni. Giovanni asks to examine the weapons and Masetto proudly and stupidly hands them over. Giovanni then beats the unarmed, surprised and bewildered Masetto unmercifully, leaving him half-dead on the ground. (As previously thought, Masetto is really only a lover – and now his intellect is suspect.) Then, as is his style, Giovanni beats a hasty retreat. Zerlina enters and is dismayed to see her battered boyfriend on the ground. She helps Masetto recover; telling him love can heal all wounds (or does love wound all heels?).

(Scene Two): A courtyard by the late Commandant's Palace (now Donna Anna's Palace). There are several doors in the wall that encloses the courtyard. It is later in the evening.

Leporello and Zerlina enter. Leporello is trying to leave before Zerlina discovers he is not Giovanni. Both of them hide as Donna Anna and Ottavio enter. Leporello again tries to leave, but as he opens a side door to escape, an angry and now bruised Masetto comes in that door with his peasant posse. Leporello is really in trouble – these folks are looking to punish Giovanni and there he is dressed and disguised as Giovanni. Talk about being at the wrong place at the wrong time. He quickly removes his master's clothing and reveals he is the servant, not the master. The group is furious with Leporello's deceit. But, they are so surprised they allow him to escape. Another hasty retreat, but this time by the servant. Ottavio vows vengeance once again for the woman he loves. He sings a famous aria (famous because all tenors desire it), *Il mio tesoro intanto* (Speak for me to my lady). The man really knows how to ingratiate himself with Donna Anna.

(Scene Three): A graveyard, the center of which has a marble statue of the Commandant. (You have to hand it to Italian know-how: They made this marble statue less than two days after the Commandant's untimely death.) It is after midnight.

Giovanni and Leporello enter from opposite directions – each one out of breath (but, of course, still able to sing). Leporello has escaped from Masetto and his posse. Giovanni has escaped from an encounter with one of Leporello's girl-friends, who for a time thought he was Leporello. This is getting confusing. To help everyone out, especially the audience, they exchange clothes and resume their proper identities.

Giovanni continues to boast. Suddenly they hear someone else's voice and their attention is drawn to the statue. Surely the voice did not come from the marble statue? Leporello, trembling, reads the inscription on the statue: "I here await that vengeance, decreed by Heaven, unto that wretch that slew me."

Giovanni laughingly, as a joke, tells his servant to ask the statue to come to his home to dine with him. Leporello fearfully obeys his master, but it takes him three tries before he is able to overcome his fear to directly address and invite the statue. (The cemetery makes Leporello believe he is in grave danger.) Giovanni laughs as his servant tells him he saw the statue nod an acceptance. Giovanni mockingly asks the statue for an answer and hears a resounding "Yes!" The unflappable Giovanni shrugs off this whole weird phenomenon and swaggers away with Leporello to go home. Leporello can't wait to get away. (Probably both of them decide to lay off the heavy grape juice for a while. Certainly they'll be staying away from grave-yards at night.)

(Scene Four): The interior of Donna Anna's inherited palace. It is early the next morning. Donna Anna and Ottavio are together in a private sitting room. She is still grieving about her father's death. She will not rest until her father's death is avenged. Ottavio wants to marry her, but Donna Anna will not even speak of marriage at such a sad time. She sings a beautiful aria, *Non mi dir* (Say no more). In other words, she only wants a buddy, not a sweetheart. (This scene doesn't seem necessary to the plot, but it gives Donna Anna a nice aria to sing and it provides a good operatic interlude.)

(Scene Five): The huge banquet hall in the interior of Don Giovanni's castle. It is the evening of the same day. A splendid feast has been prepared and a large table is set with all manner of food and drink. Giovanni is seated alone at the table heartily enjoying a sumptuous meal. Servants are scurrying about to wait on him. Hired musicians are playing for his pleasure. Giovanni is having a most enjoyable evening. Leporello watches enviously. In a bit of comic relief, Leporello sneaks a bite of pheasant, but Giovanni sees him and upbraids him for his impulsive moment of thievery.

Elvira enters, seeking an audience with her former lover. Giovanni waves away the musicians as Elvira gets on her knees and begins to plead with Giovanni. She has forgiven him and is in great sorrow for the life Giovanni is leading. She wants him to repent. Giovanni makes fun of her and gets back to eating and drinking. Leporello shakes his head and says his master has a heart of stone. (It seems Giovanni and the statue have something in common.)

A bitterly disappointed Elvira attempts to leave by one of the castle entrances, but suddenly she screams, turns completely around and rushes out a different door. Giovanni sends Leporello to see what happened. Leporello goes to the door, screams and comes back. He is unable to tell Giovanni what he saw. A knock is heard, but the terrified Leporello will not go to the door – instead, he hides under the table. (Servants are supposed to wait on tables, not under them.)

Giovanni disgustedly opens the door himself and is startled to see the marble statue of the Commandant. The statue says he has come to supper as Giovanni requested. With an air of bravado, the surprised but composed Giovanni orders Leporello to bring another dinner for his guest. Leporello ain't moving. The guest statue says he does not need mortal food. However, he demands Giovanni dine with him. The defiant Giovanni gives his hand in pledge, but refuses the statue's repeated demands to repent. Giovanni wrests his hand away as the statue tells him this is his last moment. Giovanni's answer is still no. The time for repentance is over. Roaring flames begin to envelop Giovanni as a chorus of demons tells him a worse fate is in store for him in Hell. The floor opens up as Giovanni and the statue are dragged down into Hell. Geovanni screams amid the flames and the demons claim his soul. The castle becomes calm again as the marble floor moves back into place.

From this tragic scene appear the remaining main characters a few minutes later. Leporello, with some difficulty, explains to the others what happened to his former master. He says he will seek out a new, better master. (After his unemployment benefits run out, no doubt.) The avenged Donna Anna says she will probably marry Ottavio, but wants to wait a year to relieve the grief in her heart. (Methinks Ottavio is being phased out.) The wishy-washy Elvira plans to enter a convent. Masetto and Zerlina plan to celebrate by returning home to eat. (These impressionable peasants really know how to celebrate.) All sing that the death of wicked men is always just like their life. In other words, Giovanni got what he deserved. (The end is justified, if they're mean.)

FIVE YEARS LATER
(A Fabricated and Unauthorized Epilogue)

– Donna Anna, the Commandant's daughter, remains unmarried. She is considered the most eligible maiden in Seville. After her father's statue disappeared, she went into sculpturing – not, of course, like her father.

– Don Ottavio, Donna Anna's suitor, didn't suit Donna Anna. She kept putting him off until he finally realized they had no future together. He wooed and won Donna Elvira, whom he met while they were chasing after Don Giovanni.

– Donna Elvira spent six months in a convent after Don Giovanni's timely death. She married Don Ottavio shortly thereafter. They moved to the outskirts of Madrid, where they own one of the largest wineries in all Spain.

– Leporello, Don Giovanni's faithful servant, has gone into business for himself. He found Don Giovanni's black book of addresses and has opened a profitable escort service.

– Zerlina continues her happily married life with Masetto. They have three children and she is hoping for five more. Whatever.

– Masetto did such a good job organizing the posse that chased Don Giovanni that he was appointed deputy sheriff of Seville. However, it is an administrative job. He is not allowed to carry any weapons.

– The Commandant's statue remains missing from the graveyard, although there have been sightings in other parts of Spain and Paraguay. There is a reward of 100 gold coins for its return.

***

Les Contes D'Hoffmann
(The Tales of Hoffmann)
by Jacques Offenbach
(1819-1880)
Libretto by Jules Barbier and Michel Carre
Based upon the writings of Ernst Theodor Wilhelm Hoffmann,
a German composer and author

MAIN CHARACTERS

Lindorf, a councillor of Nurenberg	*Bass*
Hermann, a student	*Baritone*
Nathanael, a student	*Tenor*
Luther, a tavern keeper	*Bass*
Hoffmann, a poet	*Tenor*
Nicklausse, Hoffmann's companion	*Mezzo-soprano*
Spalanzani, a scientist and inventor	*Tenor*
Coppelius, an inventor and rival of Spalanzani	*Baritone*
Olympia, a mechanical doll	*Soprano*
Giulietta, a courtesan	*Soprano*
Schlemil, Giulietta's lover	*Bass*
Pittichinaccio, an admirer of Giulietta	*Tenor*
Dapertutto, a sorcerer	*Baritone*
Antonia, a singer	*Soprano*
Crespel, Antonia's father	*Baritone*
Frantz, Crespel's servant	*Tenor*
Dr. Miracle, a physician and sorcerer	*Baritone*
Stella, an opera singer	*Soprano*
The Muse	*Soprano*

Place: Nurenberg, Venice, Munich
Time: Early Nineteenth Century
First Performance: Opera-Comique, Paris, France
February 10, 1881
Original Language: French

Jacques Offenbach is credited with more than a hundred operettas and is considered to be the master of French operetta in the 19th century. He managed to compose a few operas as well as all those operettas. Of all his operas, *Tales of Hoffmann* is his best known and the one most frequently performed. Yet Offenbach died before he finished *Tales of Hoffmann*. The unfinished parts were the ending in the Epilogue and some details in the *Giulietta* act. Ernest Guiraud, a fine composer and teacher, completed the opera at the request of Hoffmann's family. Offenbach must have had a good sense of humor — he was born Jacob Eberst near Cologne, Germany and sometimes he would sign his name "O.de Cologne."

The opera has undergone many changes from the time it premiered in 1881. Both arias and recitatives have been added and deleted from Offenbach's original composition. Even the original order of the acts has been changed so the Antonia act now normally follows the Giulietta act. So be it: As long as the performers don't get mixed up, the audience will never know the difference.

Tales of Hoffmann is a story of a poet who has bad luck with the ladies, but he doesn't mind sharing his failed love affairs with his drinking buddies. (When it comes to courting, though, this poet is not well versed.)

PROLOGUE

The interior of Luther's Tavern in Nurenberg. The tavern is located next door to an opera house where the prima donna Stella is starring in the opera *Don Giovanni*. (It seems drinking and singing go together in Nurenberg.) There are no customers in the tavern, only a number of tables and benches scattered about. Lindorf enters. The councillor Lindorf seems to delight in bedeviling the poet Hoffmann and he has his chance this evening. By bribery, he intercepts a love note from the diva Stella to Hoffmann. Enclosed in the note is a key to her apartment. Lindorf intends to keep the rendezvous in place of Hoffmann.

A large group of students enters the tavern, which suddenly gets very noisy and busy. The students have come in for a drink or two during an intermission of *Don Giovanni*. They are a loud and happy group and they speak glowingly of Stella's performance.

Hoffmann and his good friend Nicklausse enter, greeting their student friends and joining them for a drink. Hoffmann is in a terrible mood. When asked why, he tells them the talk of Stella, his former love, has aroused his longing for her. Evidently he knows nothing about the love note and key Stella sent him. To get Hoffmann into a better mood, his friends encourage him to lead them in a humorous drinking song, *Legend of Kleinzach*, which describes a deformed dwarf whose legs go "Clic, clac." They sing a few verses, but when Hoffmann begins singing about the dwarf's features, he gets off track and starts singing about a former mistress (she must have been a knockout). His friends wager Hoffmann is in love, but he shouldn't be embarrassed—they have girlfriends as well. Hoffmann says his spirit is troubled and implies even the deformed *Legend of Kleinzach* is better than women. (Hoffmann needs immediate medical help.)

In Hoffmann's bitter mood, he sees his adversary Lindorf at a nearby table. They take time to trade a few insults with each other. Hoffmann blames men like Lindorf for his misfortunes with women and he decides to tell his friends about those misfortunes. He tells his friends to seat themselves, to light their pipes, and to listen to the story of not one mistress, but of three mistresses who have caused him to never love again. The name of the first, he says, is Olympia.

ACT ONE

Hoffmann's tale of Olympia takes place in a richly furnished room in the home of the scientist and inventor Spalanzani. There are two doors on the sides of the room, one of which leads to Olympia's room. Spalanzani enters and peeks behind a portiere, where Olympia is apparently sleeping.[1] He refers to Olympia as his daughter, but actually Olympia is his latest invention, a mechanical doll. He has invited some friends over to show off his invention, which he hopes will make him wealthy. (She'll make a great conversation piece, batteries not

[1]A portiere is a curtain hanging across a doorway. There is absolutely no relationship between a portiere and a derriere.

included.) He leaves to prepare for the coming of his guests.

Hoffmann enters and, seeing no one around, looks behind the portiere and gazes admiringly at Olympia — he is infatuated with "her." His friend Nicklausse enters and discovers Hoffmann is crazy about Olympia (crazy about her is a good way to put it). He tries to discourage Hoffmann and hints Olympia may not be real. But Hoffmann is too enamored with her to understand what his friend is implying.

Coppelius, an inventor friend of Spalanzani, enters and induces Hoffmann to purchase a special pair of eyeglasses he says will allow the wearer to see the beauty of a woman. (Obviously these were invented by Coppelius' wife.) Hoffmann puts on his new glasses and takes another peek at Olympia. He is delighted with the results. (Must be rose-colored glasses.) Now he is even more infatuated with her. While he is enjoying the view, Spalanzani re-enters. He and Coppelius begin an argument away from Hoffmann where he can't hear them. The argument is over money. Coppelius is claiming a share of the invention because he supplied Olympia's eyes. After a brief argument, they settle on a check in the amount of 500 ducats, which Spalanzani generously writes on a bank he knows is bankrupt.

The invited guests arrive. Spalanzani "wakes" Olympia up and introduces her to his guests. Olympia is beautiful and perfectly proportioned, and the guests describe her as ravishing. (Spalanzani has done a much better job than Frankenstein did.) Hoffmann is completely smitten. Spalanzani then tells Olympia to perform for the group, which she does by singing a coloratura aria, *Les oiseaux dans la charmille* (The birds in the arbor) while Spalanzani accompanies her on a harp. It would have been a flawless performance except she winds down while singing and Spalanzani has to jump-start her so she could finish — all unnoticed or perhaps overlooked by Hoffmann. (He still has his rose-colored glasses on.)

After she finishes, Spalanzani announces dinner will be served. Hoffmann asks Olympia to accompany him, but Spalanzani intervenes and tells Hoffmann Olympia will not dine. But he tells Hoffmann he may stay and keep her company while all the others dine if he wishes to do so. Hoffmann eagerly accepts. The others leave for dinner and Hoffmann is left alone with Olympia. He makes arduous overtures to her, but she gives only one-word answers. (Many husbands would love this.) Also, she replies only when she is touched on her shoulder. When he attempts to hold her hand, she gets up abruptly and leaves the room, leaving a distraught and puzzled Hoffmann. (Many of us have had similar experiences on our first date.) Nicklausse re-enters and tries to tell his friend the truth about Olympia, but the lovesick Hoffmann doesn't listen.

Coppelius returns. Evidently it didn't take him long to find out Spalanzani had given him a hot check. He is furious and vows revenge as he slips into a side room. Meanwhile, all the guests have returned after dining. They begin to dance to some lively music. Spalanzani has returned with Olympia and he allows her to dance with a pleased Hoffmann. But, Olympia dances faster and faster until Hoffmann drops from exhaustion. Spalanzani stops the runaway Olympia and returns her to her place behind the portiere. They revive the breathless Hoffmann.

Then the sounds of smashing and crashing are heard from behind the portiere. As the guests look in that direction, a triumphal Coppelius emerges, laughing about destroying Spalanzani's invention. Sure enough, Olympia has been broken and smashed. Hoffmann finally realizes he has been in love with a mechanical doll. The crowd laughs at Hoffmann's embarrassed discomfort as they chant over and over, "He loved an automaton. He loved an automaton."

ACT TWO

Hoffmann's second tale is about the lady Giulietta, who is giving a big party at her spacious palace along the Grand Canal in Venice. Gondolas can be seen in the background as they glide along the canal. The guests are seated on cushions in an ornately decorated room singing the most celebrated music of the opera, the *Barcarole*, led by Giulietta and Nick-lausse. Hoffmann thinks the *Barcarole* is sad, and sings a livelier song in which the guests join in on the refrain.[2]

Hoffmann is infatuated with Giulietta, but her current boyfriend is Schlemil.[3] Giulietta introduces Hoffmann to Schlemil and then to Pittichinaccio, who is evidently a third suitor of Giulietta. (Hoffmann seems to have more competition for a real woman than he does for a robot.) The men are cool to each other and to avoid a quarrel, Giulietta invites the men to a card game in an adjoining room where the other guests are assembling. All leave except Hoffmann and Nicklausse. Nick-lausse warns Hoffmann about falling in love with Giulietta, but Hoffmann laughingly replies there's no way he will. He boasts the devil may damn his soul if he were to do so. (A hazardous boast — he may have to give the devil his due.) They leave to play cards.

The sorcerer Dapertutto enters. He foretells he will have Giulietta enchant Hoffmann just as he has had Giulietta enchant Schlemil. He also says Schlemil will die. He then displays a huge diamond ring on his finger. He proclaims the diamond has a fatal power irresistible to Giulietta that will cause her to be his slave and do his bidding. Dapertutto is right: Giulietta enters and immediately is attracted to the diamond ring (in some ways, Giulietta is just a normal woman). Dapertutto orders her to bring Hoffmann's reflection to him, just as she brought Schlemil's image to him. If his reflection is captured, his soul will be lost. She agrees to do so (actually, upon reflection, she agrees to do so). The pleased Dapertutto leaves.

Hoffmann re-enters. He is ready to leave the party as he has lost all his money at cards. (Hoffmann's card-playing skills evidently match his courting skills.) However, when he starts

---

[2] A *Barcarole* is not a Christmas song sung in a pub; it is a Venetian boat song with alternating strong and weak beats that suggests the rowing of a boat.

[3] Schlemil is really the guy's name, not "schlemiel," which means chump. To get the story straight: There is only one Schlemil, but all of Giulietta's boyfriends are schlemiels.

to leave, Giulietta makes a pass at him and in a few minutes totally captivates him (Hoffmann is easy). Hoffmann vows to never leave her side even though Giulietta warns him Schlemil will be jealous. Giulietta wants more than his vowed companionship. She hands him a mirror and asks for his reflection. He agrees she may have it, thinking it is merely a foolish whim of hers.

The card game is over. The guests return, headed by Nicklausse, Schlemil and Pittichinaccio. Dapertutto is with them. Schlemil realizes Giulietta and Hoffmann have been a little bit too friendly and confronts Hoffmann. Hoffmann is also confronted by Dapertutto, who tells him he looks pale and to look at himself in a mirror. When he looks in the mirror the horrified Hoffmann realizes he has lost his reflection.[4] (Hoffmann is more than pale; he's not even a shadow of his former self.) If that's not enough, Hoffmann is being urged by Nicklausse to leave before Giulietta bewitches him. (Sorry, Nicklausse, it's too late.)

Giulietta bids her guests goodnight and Schlemil escorts them away. She then retires to her apartment, but not before telling Hoffmann that Schlemil has a key to her apartment. Hoffmann is there to greet Schlemil when he returns to the palace, although Dapertutto remains in the background. Schlemil asks why Hoffmann is still there and Hoffmann replies he wants the key Schlemil has. Schlemil will not give up the key without a fight and draws his sword. Hoffmann is unarmed, but Dapertutto magnanimously provides his own sword to Hoffmann. It is a short fight; Schlemil falls mortally wounded and Hoffmann immediately retrieves the key. The grinning Dapertutto retrieves his sword.

The triumphant Hoffmann rushes to Giulietta's room to collect his prize, but she is not there. She appears in a gondola in the background with her latest suitor, Pittichinaccio (she probably liked his name better). Hoffmann reappears and is astonished to see the mocking Giulietta in the arms of another. Giulietta tells Dapertutto that Hoffmann is his property now

[4] Mirror, mirror on the wall … I don't see myself at all.

— she is no longer interested in him. Giulietta and Pittich-inaccio laugh at the distraught Hoffmann as they glide away on their gondola. (Giulietta may be on the canal, but Hoffmann is up the creek.) Hoffmann can only grit his teeth in anger and disbelief as Nicklausse leads him away.

ACT THREE

Hoffmann's third thwarted love story is about Antonia. She is singing and playing the clavichord in the music room at the home of her father, Crespel, in Munich. A large portrait of her mother, a famous singer, dominates the rear wall between two doors in the room. Antonia is singing a sad song because she misses the one she loves. The one she loves is Hoffmann, but her father has moved her to Munich to escape his advances. The luckless Hoffmann finally has a girl who loves him, but he can't get along with her father. Crespel enters and begins to fuss at her because she has broken her promise that she will not sing. She said she feels compelled to sing because she believes she has inherited her mother's voice and when she sings, her mother lives again. Crespel implores her to not sing anymore.

As she leaves, she promises she will not sing again, although she doesn't understand why her father wants her to stop singing. Antonia has her mother's beautiful voice, but she also has the symptoms of tuberculosis that took her mother's life. Crespel is concerned singing will worsen her dreaded disease. (Some of us have also been warned it would be unhealthy for us to sing.) Crespel doesn't like Hoffmann so he even blames Hoffmann for aggravating her condition.

Crespel calls loudly for his old, deaf servant, Frantz, and tries to tell him to admit no one. He has heard Hoffmann followed them to Munich and will attempt to visit Antonia. He does not want Hoffmann anywhere near Antonia. Crespel tries several times to get his message across, but Frantz's hearing is so bad he doesn't understand. A frustrated Crespel stomps out of the room. Frantz is used to Crespel's bad moods; he believes his master is a big grouch. He sings his life would be unbearable if not for the fact he can sing and dance so well. He proceeds to entertain himself with a vigorous dance that leaves him on the floor exhausted. Frantz is not a good judge of talent.

Hoffmann and Nicklausse enter. Hoffmann and Frantz greet each other as old friends. Hoffmann asks about Antonia. The deaf Frantz says his master has gone out. Hoffmann laughs at the misunderstanding and says Frantz is deafer than last year. Frantz responds by saying he is honored and he is very well. Hoffmann sees this conversation is going nowhere. Frantz finally leaves while saying how overjoyed Crespel will be to see Hoffmann. (Good help must be hard to find.)

Antonia has evidently heard Hoffmann's voice and rushes in to embrace him. Nicklausse decides three's a crowd and leaves. Hoffmann and Antonia are happy together and talk about getting married tomorrow. They talk about her love for music and she tells him her father doesn't want her to sing anymore. But, she wants to sing for him and she does (so much for keeping her promise). They sit together at the clavichord and they sing of their love for each other. As they conclude their duet, Antonia clutches her heart and almost faints. The concerned Hoffmann asks her what is wrong. She responds nothing is wrong. The sound of someone coming interrupts their conversation and Antonia runs to her bedroom. Hoffmann decides to hide so perhaps he can find out the mystery of her illness.

Crespel enters followed by Frantz, who says Dr. Miracle has arrived. (This is before our time — imagine a doctor making a house call.) Dr. Miracle enters and faces an angry Crespel. He blames Miracle for killing his wife with his medication. Dr. Miracle ignores Crespel's anger. (Dr. Miracle is a sorcerer and the personification of the devil.) He slyly claims he is there to see if the disease that claimed Crespel's wife has progressed further in Antonia. Hoffmann, still in hiding, now understands the seriousness of her illness.

Crespel orders Miracle to leave, but instead Miracle gestures toward Antonia's bedroom. The bedroom doors open by themselves. Continuing to gesture, Miracle acts as though an invisible Antonia comes through the doors and seats herself by him. He acts like he is taking her pulse and then commands her to sing. Crespel is beside himself throughout this whole demonstration and violently opposes her singing. However, from the bedroom comes the sound of her singing. Miracle then acts like the invisible Antonia is returning to her room. Miracle gestures and the bedroom doors close. Now Miracle proclaims to Crespel his medicine can save her, but Crespel angrily disagrees. Repeatedly, Miracle tells him his medicine can save her, but Crespel continues to reject him, believing Miracle is an assassin, not a doctor. The worried, eavesdropping Hoffmann totally agrees with the assassin assessment. Finally, Crespel pushes the doctor out the door and they leave together.

When it comes to courting, this poet is not well versed.

Hoffmann comes out of hiding and Antonia comes out of her room to meet him. He does not tell her what he knows, but he does request her to give up her singing. She does not understand why he has become an ally of her father, but she agrees to not sing again. Afraid that her father will return, he leaves, promising to return shortly.

Dr. Miracle re-enters as Hoffmann leaves.[5] Miracle asks Antonia how she can give up her talent and love for singing. He says Hoffmann is robbing her of her destiny and he will eventually be unfaithful to her. (Hoffmann probably shouldn't use Dr. Miracle as a character reference.) In her quandary, she sobs for help — even invoking the name of her beloved mother. Taking advantage of her love for her mother, Miracle causes the mother's portrait to illuminate and from it Antonia hears the voice of her mother calling to her (is this the 19th-century version of a picture show?) and telling Antonia to use her talent to sing. Miracle picks up a violin and plays it madly while also encouraging Antonia to sing. A dramatic trio takes place until Antonia falls on the sofa, dying from her exertion. The eerie light from the portrait dies down as the laughing Miracle leaves the room.

Crespel rushes in and embraces Antonia. She says a few words about her mother calling her, and then dies in his arms. Hoffmann enters and rushes to Antonia's side. Crespel blames Hoffmann for causing her death and attacks Hoffmann with a knife. Nicklausse arrives in time to prevent Crespel from striking Hoffmann. The devastated Hoffmann calls for a doctor — and, of course, Dr. Miracle re-enters. Miracle delights in taking Antonia's pulse and pronouncing her dead as Crespel and Hoffmann weep.

EPILOGUE

Back in the tavern, Hoffmann tells his companions he has completed his three stories of failed love. His friends were so interested in his stories that they stayed to listen to him rather than return to the opera following its intermission. Also, the opera has just ended. Hoffmann and his friends hear the audience in the opera applauding the end of the opera and acclaiming Stella's performance. Nicklausse rises to tell the

[5] Frantz is not doing his job. Maybe Crespel needs to try "An apple a day …"

tavern group he now realizes Hoffmann's three women are really just one — they all represent and are part of his love for Stella. Nicklausse proposes a toast to Stella, but this just angers Hoffmann and he warns Nicklausse to not repeat her name again. (Nicklausse seems to represent the good friend we don't listen to or appreciate.)

Hoffmann is left alone in a drunken stupor as the others leave to continue drinking and singing in an adjoining room. An eerie light glows around Hoffmann and a Muse appears. She tells Hoffmann to forget these failed love affairs and be true to his genius as a poet. She tells him he will achieve greatness. (Whatever Hoffmann has been drinking seems to be working.) He seems to understand, but shortly falls forward, consumed by his evening of drinking.

Stella enters and inquires of Nicklausse if Hoffmann is asleep. The truthful friend of Hoffmann responds he is not asleep, just dead drunk. Lindorf appears —everything has worked according to his plan. Hoffmann is drunk and cannot keep Stella's request for a date. In fact, Hoffmann never even found out about Stella's note to him. Lindorf takes Stella's arm and they leave together. Before she leaves, Stella takes a flower from her bouquet and throws it at the feet of Hoffmann. (This is Stella's version of a "Dear John" letter.) Hoffmann can now tell four stories of failed love instead of just three.

FIVE YEARS LATER
(A Fabricated and Unauthorized Epilogue)
– Lindorf, Hoffmann's adversary, was dropped by Stella after their first date. His wife left him one week later for Fritz, who was playing Don Giovanni in *Don Giovanni*. Lindorf has not remarried. He spends his nights at Luther's playing darts.

– Stella is still the prima donna of the opera scene. She hasn't missed a beat, but she does miss Fritz — misses him a lot.

– Hermann and Nathanael, student friends of Hoffmann, are still going to school. They have trouble studying — it's too noisy in the tavern.

– Luther still owns and manages the most popular tavern in town. He is thinking about opening a discotheque.

– Hoffmann has succeeded in the field of poetry as the Muse predicted. However, he has gone from four stories of failed love to six stories of failed love. He refuses to discuss the latest two with anyone, even while drinking.

– Nicklausse, Hoffmann's friend and companion, hasn't seen Hoffmann since marrying Gertrude, a woman's lib leader. She doesn't listen to him either.

– Spalanzani, the inventor of Olympia, invented a motorized transportation vehicle. His friends convinced him it would never sell because no one knew how to drive.

– Coppelius, the inventor who developed the eyes for Olympia, patched up his difficulties with Spalanzani and invented the headlights for Spalanzani's vehicle.

– Olympia, the mechanical doll, was sold to a scrap metal dealer.

– Giulietta, the woman Hoffmann killed for, is on probation for operating a gambling house without a license. Her diamond collection is the talk of Venice.

– Pittichinaccio, the apparent winner of the Giulietta sweepstakes, never returned from a gondola ride with her after a brief courtship.

– Dapertutto, a sorcerer, inadvertently said the wrong incantations and is now a frog that lives by the Grand Canal in Venice.

– Crespel, Antonia's father, opened a music shop, where he sells and maintains musical instruments of all types. He allows people to smoke in his shop, but they are not allowed to sing or even whistle.

– Frantz, Crespel's deaf servant, works for Crespel in his music shop. Crespel put him in charge of all customer complaints.

– Dr. Miracle, the physician and sorcerer, was placed under arrest for malpractice and drug smuggling. At his deposition, he muttered a few words starting with "Abra" and suddenly disappeared.

– The Muse who appeared to Hoffmann is now the dean of the Nurenberg liberal arts college. She likes the work, hates the hours.

***

Tosca

By Giacomo Puccini
(1858-1924)
Libretto by Giuseppe Giacosa and Luigi Illica
Based on the play by Victorien Sardou of the same name

MAIN CHARACTERS

Floria Tosca, an opera singer	*Soprano*
Mario Cavaradossi, a painter	*Tenor*
Baron Scarpia, the chief of the Roman police	*Baritone*
A Sacristan	*Baritone*
Cesare Angelotti, deposed Consul of the Roman Republic	*Bass*
Spoletta, a police agent	*Tenor*
Sciarrone, Baron Scarpia's orderly	*Bass*
A Jailer	*Bass*
A Shepherd boy	*Soprano*
Roberti, a torturer	*Silent role*

Place: Rome
Time: June 1800
First Performance: Teatro Constanzi, Rome; January 14, 1900
Original Language: Italian

Giacomo Puccini composed *Tosca* to a libretto written primarily by Giuseppe Giacosa. Puccini almost missed the opportunity to do *Tosca*. He wanted the operatic rights immediately after the play's premiere in 1889, but it took nine years and a rejection by the composer Alberto Franchetti (who seems to be missing in the list of notable composers) before he was able to get those rights. And then the librettist was against the project because he said there was too much plot. (Yep, we wouldn't want to have an opera with too much plot, would we?) But finally, everything came together and it was a hit from day one. Having the premiere in Rome was a nice touch since the setting of the opera is in Rome.

Tosca is set during the time when Rome was torn by political strife between the Bonapartists and the Monarchists. The Bonapartists had established a Roman Republic in Rome in

February 1798, but the monarchists ousted their new republic in September 1799. After that time, any one in Rome found to be a Republican sympathizer faced charges of treason. The events in the opera take place during the time the purge of the republic sympathizers was in effect.

Tosca is a typical Puccini opera – most of the main characters die before it's all over, so don't get emotionally attached to any of them. Also, tend not to believe what the main characters say because deceit and falsehoods rule the day (and the night, for that matter).

ACT ONE

The interior of the Church of Saint'Andrea della Valle. The entrance to the Attavanti Chapel is on the right. On the left is an easel with a large canvas covered with a piece of cloth. Painter's tools are scattered about the easel.

Angelotti enters. He has just escaped from prison, where he had been held as a political prisoner. He looks wildly around the room, fearing he might be discovered. Seeing he is alone, he hurries over by a holy water basin and finds a key that had been hidden there by a confederate. With his discovery of the key comes a huge sigh of relief. He takes the key to the chapel door, unlocks it, and disappears into the interior of the chapel after locking the door behind him.

His exit was none too soon. The Sacristan, keeper of the church's ceremonial equipment, enters and begins to perform his morning chores. Shortly thereafter, Cavaradossi enters, greets the Sacristan, and goes to the easel. He uncovers the canvas of an unfinished portrait of the Magdalen he has been painting. Cavaradossi's painting of the Magdalen portrays her as a beautiful woman with blue eyes and golden hair. (Cavaradossi may have gotten her mixed up with Goldilocks.) The Sacristan sees the portrait and gasps in surprise. He tells Cavaradossi he knows that woman – he sees her when she comes to worship there. Cavaradossi agrees. He says she is so lost in worship when she comes to church he has been able to paint her portrait without her knowledge. Cavaradossi glories in his painting (most artists aren't humble) and the beauty of the woman. He sings the aria *Recondita armonia* (Strange harmony) as he compares the beauty in his painting to his beloved Tosca. While he is singing, the Sacristan merely shrugs his shoulders and mumbles aloud several times, "Once they get painted, they all get acquainted." (No doubt a reference to painted women in general.) After Cavaradossi finishes singing, the Sacristan provides him a basket of food although Cavaradossi says he is not hungry. Then the Sacristan leaves, to the relief of Cavaradossi, who wishes to be left alone while he paints.

His solitude does not last long. Angelotti has heard the Sacristan leave, so he comes out of the chapel looking for food. The two men startle each other when they realize they're not alone. But when they recognize each other, they embrace as old friends. Learning that his friend has escaped from prison, Cavaradossi immediately locks the outside door to the church and says he will help him. A voice outside calling "Mario!" interrupts them. Cavaradossi gives Angelotti his gift basket of food and has him return to his hiding place in the chapel.

Cavaradossi realizes the voice calling him is his beloved Tosca and he opens the church door to embrace her. Tosca is perturbed because Cavaradossi had taken so long in unlocking the door for her. (She may be afraid her artist boyfriend is giving her the brush-off.) In fact, she thinks he may be hiding a rival girlfriend. He manages to allay her suspicions and they talk of how much they love each other. They plan to meet that night after her operatic performance. As Tosca is about to leave, she notices the beautiful woman in the painting and immediately becomes jealous again. She identifies the woman as L'Attavanti and accuses Cavaradossi of being unfaithful. Again, Cavaradossi calms her fears and tells her he's never met L'Attavanti. He's merely painted her portrait when she comes there to worship. Tosca accepts his explanation, embraces Cavaradossi, and leaves. (Cavaradossi may have a budding career as a diplomat.)

Cavaradossi beckons Angelotti from his hiding place. Angelotti reveals to Cavaradossi that the confederate who left the key for him is his sister, L'Attavanti – the same L'Attavanti who is Cavaradossi's unsuspecting model. (Interesting that Cavaradossi didn't recognize his good friend's beautiful sister.) Angelotti also says his sister did more than just leave him a key – she also left him an entire lady's wardrobe which he can use as a disguise. (Let's hope it's a disguise – not just a different dress and purse.) Cavaradossi gives Angelotti his key to his villa and tells him to take the lady's wardrobe and go to his villa and wait for him. Suddenly they hear a cannon shot from the fortress. It's the signal that Angelotti's escape has been discovered. They hurriedly leave the church for the sanctuary of Cavaradossi's villa.

The Sacristan enters with a group of unruly choirboys (there is no other kind). He tells the choirboys he has heard a report that Napoleon's army has been defeated in the Battle of Marengo. In honor of that defeat, he continues, there will be a great celebration in the church that evening climaxed by a beautiful *Te Deum* (a liturgical Christian hymn of praise to God). The choirboys begin their own celebration by shouting and singing.

The boys become quiet in a hurry when the feared Baron Scarpia, the chief of the Roman police, enters with a group of his men. (Not only is Scarpia a scary person in secular society – in the church he's a holy terror.) The Sacristan attempts to leave with the boys, but Scarpia makes him stay and answer his questions. While giving the Sacristan the third degree, Scarpia has his men search all corners of the church and chapel in search of Angelotti. Of course, Angelotti is no longer there, but the shrewd Scarpia finds clues that suggest he must have been there earlier. There is the clue that the chapel door was unlocked and Cavaradossi had no key. There is the empty food basket that was found inside the chapel, yet Cavaradossi said he was not hungry. Then, they find a woman's fan that could have been left by an accomplice. The fan has L'Attavanti's emblem on it – and Scarpia notices the painting of L'Attavanti on the easel. He comments to himself that this fan may be to him what a handkerchief was to Iago.[1] What good fortune, he is thinking – Tosca's artist lover may be involved with the escaped prisoner, and, even if he's not, he can cause Tosca to be jealous and have her for himself.

A crowd begins to gather in the church to celebrate the *Te Deum*. Tosca enters, looking for Cavaradossi. Scarpia, feigning kindness and helpfulness, talks to her. He shows her the fan and says he found it near the easel. He implies the painter and his girlfriend must have been surprised and she must have dropped her fan in her haste to get away. Tosca recognizes the emblem on the fan as L'Attavanti's and she immediately jumps to the conclusion Scarpia wants her to. She leaves the church in tears, perhaps to go to Cavaradossi's villa to check up on him. Scarpia sends Spoletta, one of his henchmen, to follow her. While their conversation was taking place, the music of the *Te Deum* had begun. Scarpia begins to gloat excitedly as he foresees Angelotti going to the gallows and Tosca coming to his arms. As the music of the *Te Deum* reaches its climax, Scarpia loudly exclaims that Tosca makes him forget God!

ACT TWO

Scarpia's upper room in the Palace Farnese. It is night. Scarpia is seated at the table having his evening meal. Music is heard from the Queen's party on the floor below. Spoletta enters and nervously reports they were unable to find Angelotti. Scarpia is enraged. Spoletta attempts to appease Scarpia by telling of Cavaradossi's arrest for his defiance. It works. Scarpia is pleased about Cavaradossi's arrest and orders Spoletta to bring him there along with a judge and a man named Roberti. (The judge's presence is just window dressing.)

---

[1] The reference here is to Shakespeare's *Otello*, where Iago used a handkerchief (and implied hanky-panky) to break up a happy Marriage between Otello and Desdemona. What we have here is one fictional character referencing another fictional character.

Cavaradossi expresses his outrage about being arrested. He is fit to be tied – and he will be shortly. Scarpia ignores Cavaradossi's anger, accusing him of feeding, clothing, and hiding Angelotti. Cavaradossi denies all charges. At this point, Tosca enters and rushes to the side of Cavaradossi. Cavaradossi whispers to Tosca to tell them nothing. Scarpia orders that Cavaradossi be taken away to an adjacent room to obtain his deposition. Roberti is to go with them "to use the standard procedure." It turns out Roberti is the designated torturer – nice standard deposition procedure.

Tosca is fearful, but Scarpia acts like a concerned friend to her. He brings up L'Attavanti's fan again and tries to make Tosca suspicious and jealous. Tosca doesn't fall for his ploy this time. Failing with the nice-guy approach, Scarpia takes a different tactic. He describes what is happening to Cavaradossi as a result of the so-called deposition. Cavaradossi has been tied hand and foot (he was fit to be tied, remember?) and a steel-pointed ring has been placed over his temples. Roberti pulls the ring tight every time Cavaradossi fails to answer a question. The steel points dig into Cavaradossi's head, causing him much bleeding and pain. Tosca pleads with him to stop the torture and it is stopped temporarily. But when she fails to tell Scarpia where Angelotti is hiding, the torture begins anew. Now Scarpia escalates the attack on Tosca's emotions. He has the "deposition" door opened; such that Tosca can hear the screams and moans of her beloved Cavaradossi as he is being tortured. Tosca breaks down; she can no longer stay quiet. She reveals the hiding place in a quiet, sobbing voice to Scarpia. Scarpia dispatches some men to arrest Angelotti and he orders the torture of Cavaradossi to stop. A bleeding, unconscious Cavaradossi is brought in from the torture chamber. Tosca rushes to his side and warmly embraces him. He regains consciousness only to learn Tosca has betrayed their friend. For the first time, Cavaradossi acts defeated. And, for the first time, he is angry with Tosca.

Sciarrone, who is evidently in charge of bad news, barges into the room with surprising and dreadful news for Scarpia.

The earlier report that Bonaparte's army had been defeated was in error. Actually, Bonaparte has soundly defeated their troops instead. (Well, anybody can make a little mistake.) Cavaradossi takes new courage from that bit of news. He defies the foreign oppressors. He calls Scarpia a tyrant and a murderer. (There goes Cavaradossi's career as a diplomat.) Scarpia does not take kindly to Cavaradossi's words. He sentences him to death on the scaffold and orders him removed from his sight. (And there goes Cavaradossi's career as anything, except perhaps as a martyr.) Tosca clings to Cavaradossi, but Scarpia pulls her away as Cavaradossi is taken from the room. Tosca is downcast, but she tries another approach. She tries to bribe Scarpia with money for Cavaradossi's life. Scarpia laughs – he can't be bribed with money. What Scarpia wants is instant passion – he wants Tosca. Tosca withdraws from his advances. She pours out her anguish in the aria *Vissi d'arte* (I lived for my art), describing how she has lived a life of goodness, but now it seems God has deserted her. Scarpia merely laughs at her pain and anguish.

A drum roll is heard as an execution is announced. Spoletta enters and reports Angelotti is dead; he has killed himself. He also reports what the drum roll has already implied – the execution of Cavaradossi will proceed as instructed. Tosca sees she has little choice. She sadly gives in to Scarpia in order to stay the execution and save her beloved's life. After verifying that Tosca will submit to him, Scarpia changes the method and plan of execution. He says he never pardons anyone, but what he will do is set up a sham firing squad that will make it appear Cavaradossi is executed. (After all, it would be difficult to have a sham beheading.) The firing squad will be equipped with blank cartridges for their rifles. When the squad fires, Cavaradossi is to fall down as if dead. Spoletta leaves to carry out Scarpia's orders.

Tosca demands Scarpia give her a safe passage letter that will give her and Cavaradossi freedom to leave the country after the sham execution is over. The now generous Scarpia agrees to do so. He writes the note and puts his official seal on it. He is ready to possess Tosca and in a moment of passion holds his arms out to embrace her. Tosca has a surprise for him. She has concealed a knife behind her back. As Scarpia draws near to embrace her, she stabs him. He is able to say a few dying words, [2] but he collapses as Tosca stands victoriously over him. Tosca retrieves the letter of safe passage and hides it in her bodice. She puts candles by the body of Scarpia and sets a crucifix on his chest. She leaves quietly, closing the door behind her.

ACT THREE

The roof of the Castel Sant'Angelo prison. On one side is a chair, a desk, writing utensils, a ledger and a lantern. On the other side is a trap door. It is just before dawn. In the distance a shepherd boy is heard singing as he tends to his flock.

A jailer enters through the trap door and seats himself by the desk. Soon afterward, a small contingent of soldiers arrives, escorting Cavaradossi. The jailer opens a ledger and registers the condemned Cavaradossi. He tells Cavaradossi he has an hour to live and asks if he wishes to have a priest. (What, no last meal?) Cavaradossi tells the jailer he wishes only to write a letter to one he loves. He bargains with the jailer to accept a ring in exchange for letter-writing privileges. Cavaradossi begins to write. However, he is overcome with emotion on memories of Tosca. He stops writing and sings the poignant aria *E lucevan le stelle* (And the stars shone) as he recalls the beautiful times that they had together. He stops singing and buries his face in his hands.

Tosca enters. Spoletta has brought her to the prison. She excitedly shows Cavaradossi the letter of safe passage and tells him all the events that have transpired. It is difficult for him to believe she killed Scarpia. He is overjoyed thinking how they will be free and together again. She tells him how the sham execution is to work and implores him to fall as if dead when the firing squad shoots their blanks. She worries his acting

[2] In a gangster movie, he would say something like, "Give dis watch to me mudder."

will not be good or he might move too quickly after he falls. (That will not be a problem.) He assures her he will not move until he hears her call.

Tosca had reached her jumping-off point

The jailer enters and escorts Cavaradossi to the platform where the firing squad awaits. Tosca stations herself so she can see Cavaradossi as he stands by the wall across from the firing squad. Cavaradossi smilingly refuses the offer of a blindfold. The officer readies the firing squad, and then lowers his saber as the signal for them to fire. Cavaradossi slumps to the ground. The firing squad sergeant moves forward with a pistol to administer the *coup de grace*. Spoletta stops the sergeant from using the pistol. The squad falls in line and is marched out of the area by Spoletta. Tosca rushes down by the fallen Cavaradossi and tells him all the soldiers are gone – he can get up now. Cavaradossi doesn't move. Tosca is horrified to learn the execution was real and not a sham as she had been promised.

Cavaradossi is dead. She throws herself on his lifeless body and sobs uncontrollably. She hears shouts nearby exclaiming Scarpia has been murdered and Tosca is the murderer. Spoletta and Sciarrone rush in and exclaim they see the murderer and they will make her pay for it. They move to seize her, but she violently pushes them away and escapes their clutches. Still sobbing, she runs to a parapet and throws herself over it to her death. She evidently had reached her limit of endurance. (One might say she had reached her jumping-off point.) The shocked Spoletta and Sciarrone can only stare down from the parapet at her broken body below.

FIVE YEARS LATER
(A Fabricated and Unauthorized Epilogue)

– The Sacristan continues to maintain custody of the church's ceremonial equipment. He influenced the church council to prohibit painters from utilizing the church's facilities.

– Spoletta, the police agent, was reassigned to the traffic division. Last year he received an award for handing out the most traffic violations in Rome.

– Sciarrone, Baron Scarpia's orderly, was involuntarily inducted into the army and sent to the front lines. He went AWOL shortly thereafter and has been officially listed as a deserter for three years.

– The Jailer decided procuring material for the prisoners could be very profitable. He was right. He has a brisk business going and expects to retire in two more years.

– The Shepherd boy is taking voice lessons and plans to sing professionally.

– Roberti, the torturer, would like to change professions, but his ballet lessons didn't work out. An aptitude test suggests he would be an excellent physical therapist.

POSTSCRIPT

There are two anecdotes about the last act in *Tosca* worth repeating, both having to do with Tosca leaping to her death from the prison parapet.

The most oft-told story is called the bouncing Tosca. The stagehands wanted to ensure the singer would not be hurt when she jumped to her stage death, so they replaced the mattresses that would normally break her fall with a trampoline. When Tosca jumped and hit the trampoline, she appeared a few times from above and behind the wall to the amused and appreciative audience.

The second incident occurred by a misunderstanding between the stage director and a crew of temps hired as soldiers. There was no rehearsal and the director told the temps to exit with the principals. When Tosca, the last principal on stage, leapt over the wall, the dutiful soldiers all jumped after her. What an ending!

***

Turandot

By Giacomo Puccini
(1858-1924)
Libretto by Giuseppe Adami and Renato Simoni
Based upon Friedrich von Schiller's
version of the play by Count Carlo Gozzi

MAIN CHARACTERS

Altoum, the Emperor	*Tenor*
Turandot, daughter of the Emperor Altoum	*Soprano*
Timur, an exiled Tartar King	*Bass*
Liu, a young slave girl	*Soprano*
Calaf, the Unknown Prince, son of Timur	*Tenor*
Ping, the Grand Chancellor	*Baritone*
Pang, the General Purveyor	*Tenor*
Pong, the Chief Cook	*Tenor*
A Mandarin	*Baritone*
The Prince of Persia	*Tenor*
Pu-Tin-Pao, the executioner	*Silent role*

Place: Peking, China
Time: Legendary
First Performance: Teatro La Scala, Milan; April 25, 1926
Original Language: Italian

Before he died, Puccini was able to complete all of Turandot except for the final scene. His young composer friend, Franco Alfano, completed the opera from sketches and notes left by Puccini. The premiere of *Turandot* did not include Alfano's ending. Arturo Toscanini, who conducted the opera's premiere, ended the opera prematurely at the point where Puccini's original composition ended. It is reported Toscanini laid down his baton and turned to the audience saying, "Here the Master laid down his pen." It's unfortunate the stopping point was right after the most tragic part of the opera. Supposedly, no one asked for his money back — and, too bad, they really didn't find about the happy ending until later.

Turandot is the story of an infatuated, obsessed Prince who risks his head to win the hand of a beautiful, but cold-hearted Princess. (Love is risky, no matter what body parts are involved.)

ACT ONE

It is sunset on a square in Peking, China. Massive bastions are in the background, completely enclosing the rear of the square. On one side is a high covered portico, ornately sculptured, supported by large pillars. A large gong is suspended from two arches at the foot of the portico. On the other side in the background there are huge gates opening into the square.

These are men who definititely have an axe to grind

A large crowd has gathered in the square; they are quietly listening to the words of a royal decree being read by a Mandarin.[1] It is a death decree. The decree states a person of royal blood may win the hand of the beautiful princess, Turandot, the Chaste, by solving three enigmas or riddles she will ask. The bad news, however, is the suitor who bids for her and fails to solve the three riddles will have his head removed from his body. (Talk about falling in love and losing your head.) There already have been some losers. As evidence, in the background on the bastions, there are a number of poles upon which are the severed heads of the beheaded. (Turandot's headquarters?) The Prince of Persia is the latest loser. He tried, but he couldn't answer the riddles. The decree states he is to be executed.

[1] Mandarin is a variety of orange, but our Mandarin is an important Chinese bureaucrat and not at all fruity.

The crowd is excited and clamors for the executioner, Pu-Tin-Pao.[2] They attempt to invade the bastion where the executioner resides. The imperial guards call the crowd "Dogs" (Peking-ese?) and brutally push them back. In the melee, an old blind man falls to the ground and is in danger of being trampled. His slave girl companion cries out for help and a young man comes to their aid. The old blind man is Timur, the deposed Tartar King. The young man is his son, Calaf. They have not seen each other in years; each thought the other dead. Talk about coincidence. (A coincidence like this can only happen in opera.) In their exile, they have been forced to hide their identity from their enemies. Calaf calls himself the Unknown Prince. No one knows Calaf's real name except Timur and the slave girl. The slave girl is Liu, who led the deposed king to safety and has helped take care of him since Timur was deposed and subsequently became blind. Liu has had an ulterior motive — she has loved Calaf from the time he smiled at her many years ago. The three of them move to a safe place away from the crowd and exchange hugs and tears.

Meanwhile, on the summit of the walls of a bastion, the executioner's assistants are seen sharpening a huge axe on a large whetstone. (These are men who definitely have an axe to grind.) The crowd has settled down, but now they are relishing (their appetite has been whetted?) the imminent execution of the Prince of Persia.

A procession approaches preceded by a group of singing children. The executioner's assistants are next, followed by priests, dignitaries, and the doomed Prince of Persia. Following the Prince is an immense man, the executioner, with the huge, freshly sharpened axe resting on his shoulder. The Prince is handsome and appears childlike. On seeing the Prince, the attitude of the fickle crowd changes from glee to pity. They cry out for mercy. Calaf leads the crowd in their call for mercy. Calaf calls for Turandot to show herself so he might curse her. As he calls out, the beautiful Princess Turandot

[2] If you're the executioner, no one will make fun of your name, even if it is Pu-Tin-Pao.

does appear on the walkway of a bastion wall. The entire crowd falls prostrate to the ground except the Prince of Persia, the executioner, and Calaf. Calaf is overcome by Turandot's beauty. It is love at first sight. He is awe-struck. Turandot acknowledges no one. There are no words of sarcasm or mercy forthcoming from her (not even a cutting remark). A deal is a deal. She motions to the executioner to proceed with the execution. The procession and the crowd move to the execution site, beyond the walls of the bastions.

Timur, Liu, and Calaf do not follow the crowd. Timur and Liu see Calaf has been smitten by Turandot and try to restrain him before he gets into trouble. Calaf frees himself from their grasp and rushes toward the gong suspended from the arches by the portico. Striking the gong is the means a man identifies himself as a suitor for the hand of Turandot. (After all, this isn't the *Gong Show* — Chuck Barris won't disqualify him.) He cries out the name of Turandot and like an echo a cry of Turandot comes from behind the bastions — it is the last, dying cry of the Prince of Persia just before he is beheaded. His cry is followed by the sound of a muffled blow of an axe, triggering the distressed cries of the crowd. Calaf hesitates, but his obsession overcomes him, and again he prepares to strike the gong.

Before Calaf can strike the gong, three masked men interivene. These three men are the Emperor's ministers: Ping, Pang, and Pong. (Were Peng and Pung out of town?) In a comical, but serious way, the ministers attempt to dissuade Calaf from striking the gong. They tell him all their graveyards are occupied. They tell him they have enough native madmen; he should go some other place to lose his head. They tell him to either leave women alone or else get 100 wives — after all, Turandot has only two arms and two legs, but with 100 wives he would have legs galore (you do the math). Turandot's serving maids interupt the ministers' pleas. The women want the ministers to be quiet so their mistress Turandot can sleep. (Her beauty sleep, no doubt.) But, the ministers ignore their request and tell the women to leave, which they do.

The ministers continue with their arguments to Calaf. Then some eerie, mysterious voices are heard out of the darkness telling of their love for Turandot. These voices are from the former suitors of Turandot who were beheaded. (Who said dead men tell no tales?) Their loss of life is emphasized when the executioner appears on the summit of the bastions. He adds to the collection of heads displayed there by planting the severed head of the Prince of Persia on a sharp spike. (Question: If he placed all the heads in a row, would he be a headliner?) And, if the gruesome reminder of severed heads is not reason enough, Timur and Liu fearfully add their dissenting voices to dissuade Calaf from striking the gong. All of them attempt to drag Calaf away, but to no avail. (They are trying to get Calaf to ... er, uh ... use his head.) Liu desperately pleads with him, *Signore, ascolta* (My lord, listen) saying his father and she will die if he stubbornly continues his quest. Calaf is moved, but replies, *Non piangere, Liu* (Do not weep, Liu) saying he is resolute in his quest.

Calaf breaks free of their grasp and flings himself against the gong. Then picking up a hammer he strikes the gong three times while he loudly yells Turandot's name. (That did it — he's in trouble now — he probably woke up the sleeping princess.) The Emperor's guards immediately rush forward to seize Calaf. They lead him away to await his enigma ceremony. Timur and Liu cling together in despair. The ministers throw their arms up in surrender and leave Calaf to his chosen fate. They exit quietly. They don't want to be around when Turandot wakes up.

ACT TWO

(Scene One): Ping, Pang, and Pong are together in a pavilion reminiscing about the good old days before Turandot. In those days things went according to ancient rules and traditions. Now, their festivities consist of three sounds of the gong, three enigmas, and one more severed head. The last several years there have been 26 of those severed heads. (This is technically called a head count.) Their reveries are interrupted by the sound of trumpets announcing the beginning of the enigma ceremony. It's game day. The ministers leave to join the ceremony.

(Scene Two): A vast square in front of the Imperial Palace. There is an enormous marble staircase leading down from the palace into the open square. There are three broad landings on the staircase where different servants of the palace are stationed. Timur, Liu, and a large crowd have gathered in the square awaiting the start of the ceremony. They look up to the top of the staircase where members of the home team are situated. Standing near the top of the stairs are eight Wise Men who are holding three sealed scrolls, which contain the solution to Turandot's enigmas. (Eight wise men for three scrolls — another union requirement?) Arriving at the head of the stairs are Ping, Pang, and Pong. Near them and seated on his throne is the very old Emperor Altoum. Calaf stands at the foot of the stairs.

Three times the Emperor speaks directly to Calaf in attempts to dissuade Calaf from continuing. Each time Calaf replies, "I crave to be put to the test!" (The Emperor probably thinks he is dealing with a craving idiot.) The Emperor finally replies, "So be it! Let thy fate be sealed!" Immediately, Turandot's women attendants proceed from within the palace and take their places on the stairs.

The Mandarin comes forth and announces the well-known ground rule: Answer the three enigmas or forfeit your head. When he has finished, the beautiful Turandot advances toward the throne. She tells Calaf the enigmas are three, death is but one. Calaf replies, "No, no! The enigmas are three, life is but one!" After he responds, she relates how a pure, innocent Princess ancestor of hers was carried off, ravaged, and killed. Turandot says she is taking revenge on all men for that outrage and has sworn no man shall ever possess her. (Other than that, she's open-minded.)

Then, impassively, with no emotion, she states the first enigma to Calaf. "At night a phantom takes flight over a humanity in gloom. It disappears at dawn to be reborn in the heart of man. Each night it is born anew to fade away at the light of day." After a short silence, Calaf confidently answers, "Yes, it is born anew — it is HOPE!" Together the Wise Men unroll the first scroll — sure enough, the answer is Hope.

The crowd murmurs and Turandot seems surprised - probably none of the other suitors ever got this far. She walks halfway down the staircase as if to bedazzle Calaf. She states the second enigma, "It spurts like a flame and is delirious. It grows cold if thy life is gone. If thou dreamest of conquest, in ardency it glows." Calaf hesitates and the crowd is afraid the underdog has lost. Turandot has a look of triumph. Suddenly, Calaf responds, "Yes, in ardency it glows within me when I look at thee — it is BLOOD!" Quickly, the Wise Men unroll the second scroll and confirm Calaf's answer is correct. The crowd cheers, which angers Turandot so much she orders the Palace guards to whip them into silence.

Now, deliberately, she comes down the stairs and towers over a kneeling Calaf as if to intimidate him. With ferocity she states the third enigma. "Ice which gives thee fire! And from thy fire ice begets! Candid and obscure! If freedom she grants thee, into greater slavery thou fallest! If as slave she accepts thee, a King thou shalt be!" Calaf does not answer. Turandot scornfully says she knows he cannot answer because he has lost. Calaf looks lost for a moment, but suddenly he jumps to his feet exclaiming, "Thou canst not escape me — my fire thaws thee — the answer is TURANDOT!" Turandot staggers back as if she has been shot. The Wise Men excitedly confirm Calaf is correct. The crowd explodes with cheers.

Turandot retreats up the stairs and throws herself at the feet of her father, the Emperor. She implores him to save her from the stranger. The Emperor replies his oath is sacred. (And, he's probably thinking, "To the victor goes the spoiled.") Turandot seems to have forgotten a deal is a deal. She argues she alone is sacred. She haughtily tells Calaf no man will ever possess her. She asks him if he wants her full of ire or reluctant like a prey. Not liking her suggested options, Calaf says he wants her ardent with love and not with hate. Then, a big surprise! Calaf gallantly releases her from the bargain even though he had staked his life and won. Then, a bigger surprise! He places his life on the line again. He tells her if she can tell him his real name before dawn then he will lay down his life. (Timur is probably now wondering about his son's IQ.) To Calaf's knowledge, no one there knows his real name except Timur and Liu: All this time he has been called either the Stranger or the Unknown Prince. The pale and shaken Turandot says nothing but gives an affirmative sign. The crowd murmurs they cannot believe Calaf would make such a proposal. The Emperor is pleased at the generosity and fear-lessness of his future son-in-law and tells him the palace is at his disposal. (It sounds like Dad is ready for the *Gong Show* to end and for his daughter to get married.) The crowd cheers at the bravery of Calaf and all anxiously await the coming of dawn.

ACT THREE

(Scene One): One of the beautiful gardens of the Imperial Palace. On one side are steps leading to a pavilion that adjoins Turandot's chambers. It is night. Calaf is reclining on the steps of the pavilion. He listens to the voices of heralds in the background proclaiming loudly, over and over, "Let no one sleep. Unless the name of the Unknown Prince is revealed before dawn, death will be the penalty." (Evidently this is Princess Turandot's incentive plan to get information.) Calaf then sings the well-known and best aria of the opera, *Nessun Dorma* (None shall sleep) that echoes the herald's proclamation, but reaffirms his resolve that his secret will not be disclosed before dawn.

A crowd of people enters the garden headed by Ping, Pang, and Pong. They approach Calaf. The ministers plead for all their lives. They tell him they will be killed. They describe how they will be tortured before they are killed. There is no response from Calaf. Then, they try another tactic. They attempt to bribe Calaf with a group of beautiful maidens. They offer him gold and gems. They say they will help him flee to regions unknown. (They obviously have a great witness-protection program.) All Calaf has to do, to get these promised rewards, is reveal his name to them before dawn. Calaf is un- moved. He is steadfast in his desire for Turandot, nothing else.

The desperate crowd moves close to Calaf in a threatening manner. Some draw their daggers. The confrontation is interrupted when a group of guards drag Timur and Liu into their midst. Ping recognizes them as companions of Calaf the day before. Calaf denies the two prisoners know anything. Excitedly, Ping fetches the veiled Turandot from her chambers and tells her the two prisoners know the name of Calaf if they would but speak. Turandot threatens Timur, but before he says anything, Liu comes forward and says Timur knows nothing. She says she is the only one who knows the name of the suitor and she will keep that secret as her sole possession. Calaf continues to deny the prisoners know anything. Ping, the crowd, and Turandot think otherwise.

The soldiers render Calaf helpless by shackling him. Then they begin to torture Liu, but it is in vain, she does not tell them his name. Turandot stops the torture momentarily and asks Liu how she is able to withstand the pain. Liu replies it is through love. The torture resumes. Liu says she will speak, but it is not to reveal Calaf's name. Instead, her aria, *Tu che di gel sei cinta* (You who are encircled in ice) tells Turandot that despite her icy heart and resistance she will voluntarily submit to the Unknown Prince. Then, catching everyone by surprise, she snatches a dagger from one of the soldiers and stabs herself. She looks at Calaf tenderly, staggers toward him, and then falls dead at his feet. Timur and Calaf are grief-stricken with the loss of their loyal friend. Turandot is merely angry. She whips the dagger-less soldier in the face. The crowd is hushed for they fear the dead girl will be a malignant spirit and bring harm to them. Some of the crowd comes forward to gently carry Liu's body away. Calaf is freed. The ministers fear the princess, but feel compassion for perhaps the first time in years.

Everyone leaves the garden except for Turandot and Calaf. Calaf tears Turandot's veil away and despite her objections kisses her passionately. (Always remove a veil before kissing some-one). Instead of being angry, Turandot is confused and cries out he has won. Calaf continues to whisper sweet nothings to her as Turandot seems to be resigned to her fate. The bewilder-ed Turandot asks him to leave and take his secret with him. Calaf feels he can trust her and they belong together. He reveals his secret, his name, to her. (Maybe Timur was right to worry about his son's IQ.) Turandot is revitalized because dawn has just arrived — and, now, she knows the name of her suitor. A moment before, she had acted defeated — now she draws herself up majestically and orders Calaf to appear before the people with her. They leave together to return to the great staircase and to the presence of the Emperor.

(Scene Two): Now all are present in front of the great staircase by the Imperial Palace where Calaf had answered the three enigmas. At the top of the staircase are the Emperor, dignitaries, the eight Wise Men, and soldiers. A huge crowd is waiting expectantly. (News travels fast in Peking — and, besides, who could sleep with all the noise the Heralds were making last night?) The three ministers spread a cloth of gold in front of Turandot as she walks up the staircase. She approaches her father and tells him she knows the name of the stranger. She looks directly at Calaf and says slowly and sweetly, "His name — is Love!" Calaf runs up the staircase and embraces a willing Turandot while the crowd cheers with joy. (Well, Timur, you didn't have to worry about Calaf's IQ after all. He found the only way to win proud Turandot's love.) A happy ending indeed — except for Liu, who was really the only virtuous person in the whole story.

FIVE YEARS LATER
(A Fabricated and Unauthorized Epilogue)
    – Altoum, the Emperor, set up a riddle contest three years ago in order to obtain a wife. The loser would not die, but only be sentenced to six months in the Emperor's kitchen. So far no one has entered.
    – Calaf, the Unknown Prince, remains the Emperor's favorite. He will replace the Emperor next year when the

Emperor retires. He gives frequent lectures on psychology.

– Turandot, daughter of the Emperor, is seldom seen in public. She is calm, gentle, and obeys her husband Calaf. She is kept busy tending to their four children: Hai, Ho, Tawn, Tow.

– The Mandarin is now responsible for all health, education and welfare issues for the Emperor. He is currently reviewing a new procedure called acupuncture, but he gives it little chance to be useful or popular.

– The Eight Wise Men are still the Emperor's advisors. They are very old. There is some concern whether all of them are still breathing.

– Timur, the father of Calaf, lives in a luxurious apartment in the Emperor's Palace. He has been assigned eight litter bearers, who transport him anywhere he wants to go.

– Pu-Tin-Pao, the executioner, is still the ambitious person that he was when he was first named executioner (he still wants to get ahead). Unemployed after the riddles were solved, he moved to Southern China and works for a royal family there.

– Ping and Pong became interested in sports and developed a new game that most of Peking is playing. The game is played on a tabletop with wooden paddles and a small hollow ball. They have tentatively called the game table tennis until they can think of a better name.

– Pang hated sports and dissociated himself from Ping and Pong. He turned his attention to culinary projects. He developed some eating utensils that are changing the eating habits of all Peking. In honor of the men who lost their heads during the riddle era, he named the utensils chopsticks.

– The Heralds have all remained in the Emperor's employment except Hoo Haw. Hoo Haw left the Emperor's staff to work as a cashier in a local food market. Hoo is a Chinese Checker. (That's a statement — not a question.)

***

La Cenerentola
(Cinderella)
by Gioacchino Rossini
(1792-1868)
Libretto by Jacopo Ferretti
Based on Charles Etienne's French libretto
for Niccolo Isouard's opera *Cendrillon* (1810)

MAIN CHARACTERS

Don Ramiro, the Prince	*Tenor*
Dandini, the Prince's valet	*Baritone*
Alidoro, the Prince's tutor and advisor	*Bass*
Don Magnifico, Cinderella's stepfather	*Bass*
Cinderella, Angelina	*Mezzo-soprano*
Clorinda, Cinderella's stepsister	*Soprano*
Tisbe, Cinderella's stepsister	*Mezzo-soprano*

Place Salerno
Time: Unspecified, but the costumes
are usually late 18th Century
First Performance: Teatro Valle, Rome, January 25, 1817
Original Language: Italian

Gioacchino Rossini composed *Cinderella* before he reached the tender age of 25 (actually, counting birthdays, he was only six – he was born on February 29). He and the librettist, Jacopo Ferretti, staged *Cinderella's* premiere only one month after they decided on the subject matter. The opera *Cinderella* is somewhat like the children's story of *Cinderella,* but there are far more differences than there are similarities. The good fairy godmother and the bad stepmother are missing in the opera, but there is a handsome prince to like and two ugly, misbehaving and selfish stepsisters to dislike. Also, this Cinderella doesn't have a glass slipper; but perhaps opera music doesn't go along with someone trying on shoes (or maybe the plot in the opera just got off on the wrong foot). Anyway, everything still works out fine in the end, as you shall see.

ACT ONE

(Scene One): A large ground-floor room in Baron Don Magnifico's castle. The room is sparsely furnished. A large fireplace dominates one side of the room. Cinderella is tending the fire for her stepfather, Baron Don Magnifico, and her two stepsisters, Clorinda and Tisbe.[1] As she works, she sings *Una volta c'era un re* (Once there lived a king), which tells of a lonely king who married a woman for her goodness and not for her wealth or status. (No doubt her favorite song.) While Cinderella is working, her two stepsisters are busy grooming themselves, which is basically a full-time job. There are no servants; Cinderella is the only one who waits on members of her stepfamily. Also, the castle is in a great state of disrepair because Don Magnifico squandered not only all of his money but also the dowry that Cinderella's father had left specifically for her. (When we say poor Cinderella, we mean poor Cinderella.)

A knock is heard at the door. Cinderella, who is also the butler, opens the door to see Alidoro, the Prince's tutor and advisor, dressed in disguise as a beggar. He is doing some surveillance work for the Prince in order to find a suitable girl for him to marry. Alidoro doesn't tell them this, but the Prince has to find his Princess right away or be disinherited. The two stepsisters tell the beggar to go away, but Cinderella says some kind words and manages to slip him some coffee and bread. The stepsisters manage to extract themselves from in front of the mirror long enough to see that Cinderella has helped the beggar. Her kindness angers them and they begin to strike Cinderella and stop only when they hear someone at their door.

Several of the Prince's courtiers enter. The courtiers announce that Prince Ramiro will arrive soon to escort the ladies to his palace for a gala ball, where he will choose the most beautiful woman to be his wife. Rather than complain

---

[1] Cinderella's real name is Angelina, but she is called Cinderella because she is always tending the fire. Of the Baron's three daughters, one could say that Cinderella is the coal-minders daughter. (With apologies to Loretta Lynn)

about inadequate notice, the stepsisters shift into high gear. They call Cinderella to bring them their fine clothes and jewelry – and be quick about it. Clorinda pitches a coin for Cinderella to tip the departing courtiers. She gives them the coin. However, she feels sorry for the disguised beggar and apologizes to him. She tells him she has no money herself and is sorry she had to give the coin to the courtiers instead of him. Alidoro tells her not to worry. He tells Cinderella that perhaps by tomorrow she will be happy.

Cinderella, now alone with her sisters, faces the full brunt of their demands for her assistance in getting them dressed for the Prince's ball. Cinderella is even fussed at and threatened by them when she dares to address them as sisters. They don't talk to her very long. Instead, they rush to their father's room to tell him the news of the ball. They argue with each other over who has the privilege of telling their father the good news.

The noise disturbs the sleep of their father, Don Magnifico, who greets them disdainfully and in his dressing gown. Before they can tell him their news, he tells them about a wondrous dream he had in the aria *Miei rampolli femminini* (My feminine offspring). He dreamt he was a very beautiful donkey with feathers that enabled him to fly to the roof of a bell tower, where the bells were pealing. But, he said, that's when their noise awoke him. No matter – he sees in the dream tremendously favorable symbolism. (As you will see, the Baron's oneirocritical talent matches his ability to manage finances and daughters.)[2] He believes a dream of pealing bells means great joy. The donkey symbolizes himself (the good Baron is making an ass out of himself), the feathers are his daughters, and the flight means farewell to his plebeian status. It's obvious to him that one of his daughters will someday become Queen and bare future Kings. Pleasant thoughts to be sure, but the good Baron is living in dreamland.

The daughters now manage to interrupt the musings of their father to tell him their news regarding the Prince's ball. Excitedly they tell him the Prince will be choosing the most

[2] This means his talent for interpreting dreams is bad.

beautiful girl to be his wife. Don Magnifico, who evidently missed the "most beautiful" criterion, grows faint with anticipation that one of his daughters will fulfill the symbolic dream he had. What a coincidence! First, the dream and now the opportunity of reality. He has Cinderella fetch him some coffee while he admonishes his daughters to not only dress smart, but to think and speak very carefully at the ball. (Well, they can dress smart, anyway.) All leave to go to their individual rooms to prepare for the ball.

Prince Ramiro enters, disguised as the Prince's valet. He startles Cinderella, who drops the empty food dishes she is carrying from Don Magnifico's room. They talk and immediately are drawn to each other by their conversation and their looks. They are interrupted when Don Magnifico, Clorinda, and Tisbe all call for Cinderella at the same time to be waited on. Cinderella leaves while the disguised Prince stays to announce to the household the Prince is arriving to escort the daughters to the ball.

Dandini, the valet disguised as the Prince, enters with his courtiers. Dandini sweet talks the stepsisters and each of them think they have already enslaved him. Don Magnifico believes the Prince's goose is cooked: He is already looking forward to his new title and his new son-in-law. Ramiro quietly tells Dandini he is overacting in his role as Prince and to get on with taking the stepsisters to the ball. All leave except the real Prince Ramiro, Don Magnifico, and Cinderella.

As Don Magnifico prepares to follow them, Cinderella approaches her stepfather and begs him to allow her to go to the ball for just one hour. He refuses. She begs for half-an-hour – or even a quarter-hour. Don Magnifico tells her to forget it or he will thrash her. A sympathetic Ramiro attempts to intercede, but when he does, Don Magnifico implies it's not any of his business. And, anyway, she's nothing but a miserable, vile servant.

Before Ramiro can reply, Alidoro enters carrying a large book in his hands. Alidoro is not disguised as a beggar now; he is dressed according to his position as the Prince's advisor.

The book he carries contains a list of all the marriageable girls in the kingdom. The list shows Don Magnifico has three daughters. Alidoro asks where the third daughter is. Cinderella attempts to volunteer that she is the third daughter, but Don Magnifico pushes her in a corner. (Some believe his action started the present day practice of "time-out" punishment for kids.) He threatens her life if she speaks out. Don Magnifico then says the third daughter died. (Don M is really afraid his misuse of Cinderella's dowry will be discovered.) After a moment of uneasy silence, all leave for the ball except for Cinderella and Alidoro.

Cinderella is distraught by her treatment, but Alidoro speaks kindly to her. He wants her to attend the ball and has already arranged for a carriage to take her there. Cinderella is skeptical. She's never seen kindness before. She argues she only has rags to wear. (Of course, this is a woman's customary complaint on being invited to a nice party.) Alidoro says he will provide her with gown and jewels. (Of course, this is not a man's normal response to the rags-to-party complaint.)[3] He tells her she will appear as a great lady, but she must not reveal who she is or where she comes from. Cinderella cannot believe this is really happening. However, she accepts her good fortune and excitedly leaves with Alidoro to prepare for her masquerade. She can't wait to wear the promised gown and jewels.

(Scene Two): A chamber in Prince Ramiro's palace. The room is elaborately furnished, a big contrast to the barren room in Baron Magnifico's castle.

Dandini enters arm-in-arm with Clorinda and Tisbe. Don Magnifico and Ramiro follow. Dandini compliments Don Magnifico on his just-completed dissertation on wine and winemaking. He sends Don Magnifico to the wine cellar with the promise he will be the Royal Wine Steward if he still has his faculties after his 30th drink. (This is Dandini's version of

[3] Yes, it is an unusual response by a man. However, here the Prince's advisor, Alidoro, is not the husband and actually he is taking the place of the absent fairy godmother (and maybe Cupid as well).

an aptitude test.) The pleased Don Magnifico leaves. Ramiro also leaves after privately instructing Dandini to find out all he can about the two stepsisters. The girls practically fight over Dandini such that he disgustedly has to disengage himself from them. (Evidently, the girls got his dander-ini up.) They separate and leave.

(Scene Three): A pavilion near the wine cellar in Prince Ramiro's palace. On one side of the pavilion there is a desk with writing materials and a number of chairs. Don Magnifico is seated at the desk, surrounded by a group of the Prince's courtiers. Don Magnifico has successfully sampled 30 casks of wine, drunk enough for three men, and hasn't staggered. The courtiers announce he has passed the test: He is now the Royal Wine Steward. Don Magnifico makes his first edict. He says it will be unlawful to mix one drop of water in wine for the next 15 years. He orders the courtiers to put his edict in writing, make 6,000 copies, and distribute it throughout the city. (Well, he didn't stagger, he didn't fall – but he's sure a bureaucrat, after all.) Don Magnifico leaves, followed by the courtiers, who are wondering how to make 6,000 copies without a copy machine.

Prince Ramiro and Dandini enter the pavilion as the others leave. Ramiro tells Dandini to report on his findings regarding the two stepsisters. Dandini says they are a mixture of insolence, capriciousness and vanity. (Otherwise, they're OK.) Ramiro is surprised at this report because Alidoro had told him one of the daughters is worthy to be his wife. Well, he wasn't interested in them anyway – let someone else marry them. But for now, the masquerade must continue until he can find the woman he wishes to marry.

Clorinda and Tisbe rush into the pavilion, interrupting the men's conversation. The sisters make overtures to Dandini. He tells them he cannot marry them both; one will have to marry a groom. The girls are distraught. They cannot imagine such a terrible fate. Ramiro and Dandini have a difficult time concealing their laughter at the girls' discomfort.

They all hear a commotion outside, and then Alidoro

enters. Alidoro tells them an unknown, veiled lady has arrived. The stepsisters are immediately anxious and jealous. Dandini bids the lady to enter and unveil herself. The mysterious lady is of course Cinderella, who is richly dressed. She enters and removes her veil. Her beauty strikes everyone, but no one recognizes her. [4] Ramiro seems particularly captivated by her attractiveness. Alidoro congratulates himself on staging this scene for his boss.

It seems Cinderella has arrived just in time for dinner. Our new Wine Steward, Don Magnifico, enters to announce a table of food and wine awaits them. He notices Cinderella and tells his daughters she is a lookalike for Cinderella. (Even after 30 drinks, Don Magnifico has better eyesight than the others.) [5] The daughters tell him to take a second look – this one is put together much better than Cinderella. Dandini interrupts them. He doesn't want any more small talk; he is ready to dine. He orders all of them to proceed to the banquet table. As an aside, he says while he is in this role as Prince, he will eat enough for four. (Most performers in this role can easily eat enough for four.)

ACT TWO

(Scene One): A chamber in Prince Ramiro's palace. After the fine meal, Don Magnifico is talking with his two daughters, Clorinda and Tisbe. They talk about the mysterious woman who looks so much like Cinderella, but they reason it couldn't possibly be her because they left her in rags at home. They rationalize they dislike Cinderella so much that they can't bear anyone who even resembles her. Besides, they're not too concerned about the mysterious woman. They are all convinced the Prince will marry either Clorinda or Tisbe – and, the father

[4] This is typical opera. No one saw through Alidoro's disguise or Cinderella's makeover. And, the Prince and his valet can change places without detection.

[5] Salerno's city codes prohibit an ophthalmologist to practice there. That law appears to be shortsighted. (Maybe this explains why no one could see through any of the disguises.)

relishes the kind of life he will enjoy when that happens. Each of the daughters still frets about finishing second and having to wed a mere groom.

After they leave the room, Prince Ramiro enters, but hides when Cinderella and Dandini enter. Alidoro enters, but he also hides before he is seen. (Evidently hide-and-seek is a favorite game in the palace.) Dandini really likes Cinderella and makes a pass at her. Cinderella tells Dandini to keep his distance because she loves Dandini's groom and she cares not for the Prince's wealth and rank. Ramiro hears her response and joyfully comes out of hiding to ask for her hand.[6] However, she keeps her promise to Alidoro and does not reveal who she is or where she comes from. She says Ramiro must seek her out and find out more about her first. Before she leaves, she gives him a bracelet that matches a duplicate she wears. (Well, Ramiro, if you can't have her hand, at least come away with her bracelet.)

After she leaves, Ramiro tells Dandini the masquerade is

If you can't have her hand, at least come away with her bracelet

[6] Ramiro hasn't put two and two together yet. He does not seem to question why this woman would love him even though to his knowledge they just met in the palace a short time ago.

over and he now assumes his true identity as the Prince. He gathers his courtiers and leaves to seek the whereabouts of Cinderella. Alidoro is pleased his plans are working so well. He leaves to ensure the Prince's carriage will have a break-down near Don Magnifico's house so Ramiro will find Cinderella. Dandini remains, mulling about being an ex-Prince when Don Magnifico excitedly comes in to find out if Dandini, as the Prince, has made his choice between his two daughters. Dandini says the choice has been made, but it is a secret and is rather bizarre. As an aside, Don Magnifico asks, "What does he want? Does he want to marry me?" (At least Don M has a sense of humor.) Then Dandini reveals his true identity. He tells Magnifico he is not a Prince, but a mere valet. Don Magnifico is shocked and surprised. He becomes angry and can-not be consoled. Dandini says he knows how shattering it can be to fall from high to low, but not to worry – at a later date he will give Don Magnifico a free shave or haircut. The ex-Prince is quite generous. Don M is underwhelmed. The ex-Prince had better keep his distance.

(Scene Two): The ground-floor room in Baron Don Magnifico's castle. Cinderella is back home again, dressed in her rags, tending the fire. She declares again how she so prefers the Prince's groom to the Prince. She knows he loves her, also. Don Magnifico and his daughters return from the ball. They speak harshly as usual to Cinderella and tell her to get busy and fix them some food. (Cinderella's probably thinking – didn't they just come from a big dinner?) Cinderella leaves to do their bidding, noting what a bad humor all of them are in.

Dandini enters and tells them the Prince's carriage has had a breakdown nearby. Don Magnifico continues to be impolite to Dandini because of his deception, but brightens up when Ramiro enters. Now that Don Magnifico knows who the real Prince is, he thinks the Prince must be there to pick one of his daughters as his wife. He yells for Cinderella to come in a hurry and bring a special chair for the Prince. Cinderella hurries in and sets the chair in front of Dandini, still thinking he is the Prince. Don Magnifico corrects her and when the real Prince turns out to be the one she loves, she is embarrassed and hides her face. Ramiro comes to her rescue. He spots the duplicate bracelet Cinderella is wearing and joyfully greets her. [7]

Clorinda and Don Magnifico haven't caught on. They tell Cinderella to leave because she insults royalty by even being in their presence. Ramiro becomes very angry that they would dare insult the one he loves. He takes Cinderella by her hand and says she will be his bride. Don Magnifico, Clorinda, and Tisbe fall over themselves laughing, thinking the Prince is joking and making fun of Cinderella. The joke is on them. Ramiro is more insistent, overwhelming Cinderella and astonishing her stepfamily members. Cinderella is overjoyed and wants to share her good fortune with her family. She attempts to embrace each of her stepfamily members, but they resist her advances. Ramiro takes Cinderella in his arms and they leave.

All follow except Clorinda, Tisbe, and Alidoro. The stepsisters still do not recognize Alidoro as the beggar – so he reminds them how they treated him when he came begging for food. He tells them their father is in great debt and they will probably spend their days in misery unless they obtain pardon from the throne. They dislike the alternatives they hear, especially the misery option. They reconcile themselves to the fact they will have to beg for pardon to one they have so mistreated and degraded. There will be a few sleepless nights ahead.

(Scene Three): The grandiose Throne Room in Prince Ramiro's palace. Prince Ramiro and Cinderella are magnificently dressed and are seated on the throne. Dandini and the courtiers are on their right. Don Magnifico is near them with downcast eyes. Alidoro enters, escorting Clorinda and Tisbe, both of whom have their faces in their hands. Don Magnifico attempts to blame his two daughters for Cinderella's treatment, but Cinderella interrupts his speech with her showpiece

[7] Rossini must have thought the bracelet was not as pedestrian as a glass slipper.

number, *Nacqui all'affanno* (Born to sorrow). She tells of her transformation and does not wish to hear any excuse or apology from her family. She implores the Prince to forgive her stepfather and stepsisters. She doesn't want them to be punished for her mistreatment. (Cinderella's too nice to rake them over the coals.) She is very happy now and wants to share her good fortune with her family. She tells them to lift their eyes and she moves forward to embrace them as daughter, sister, and friend. All agree that Cinderella is more than worthy and deserving of the throne she now has. (Of course, no one has been identified to tend the fire at the Baron's castle.) And, by the way, the Princess should now be known as Angelina, rather than Cinderella. The hero in this story has to be the Prince's advisor, Alidoro. Let's hope the Prince gives him a raise.

FIVE YEARS LATER
(A Fabricated and Unauthorized Epilogue)

– Don Ramiro, the Prince, received his promised inheritance, the Southern Kingdom, after marrying Cinderella. Two years ago he opened a very popular theme park for children called "Cindyland."

– Angelina, a.k.a. Cinderella, has never forgotten her past. Her three children are named Ashley, Cole, and Ember.

– Don Magnifico, Cinderella's stepfather, has retained his appointment as the Royal Wine Steward. Although his castle has been generously restored by the order of the Prince, he spends almost all of his time in the Royal Wine Cellar.

– Clorinda and Tisbe, Cinderella's stepsisters, are in business for themselves. They own the "Two Sisters' Beauty Shoppe" and the "Two Sisters' Merry Maid Castle Cleaning Service." Both businesses are prospering. Neither sister is married.

– Dandini, the Prince's valet, left the Prince's employment (with the Prince's approval) and went into the hair-grooming business. His products are used by the "Two Sisters' Beauty Shoppe" as well as sold over the counter. He owns the potion patent for preventing the white flaky scurf that appears on people's shoulders after they comb their hair. Originally, Dandini named those flakes Danderscurf, but later shortened the name to Dandruff, a name still used today.

– Alidoro, the Prince's tutor and advisor, is now formally addressed as Don Alidoro. He is the Prince's only consultant. For his service to the Prince, he got a significant raise in pay and a castle on the Mediterranean, where he spends most of his time. He has written several fiction books about Don Ator, a good-hearted thief and master of disguises.

– The Prince's courtiers remain quite busy writing, copying and distributing additional edicts from Don Magnifico, the Wine Steward. The staff has grown much larger during the past five years and the Prince may have to raise taxes accordingly.

***

Samson et Dalila

(Samson and Delilah)
By Camille Saint-Saëns
(1835-1921)
Libretto by Ferdinand Lemaire
Based on the story in Judges in the Old Testament

MAIN CHARACTERS

Samson, a Hebrew leader chosen by God	*Tenor*
Delilah, a Philistine woman who worships Dagon	*Mezzo-Soprano*
High Priest of Dagon	*Baritone*
Abimelech, Satrap of Gaza	*Bass*
An Aged Hebrew	*Bass*
The Philistines' Messenger	*Tenor*

Place: Gaza in Palestine
Time: Around 1150 BC
First Performance: Hoftheater, Weimar, December 2, 1877
Original Language: French

The opera *Samson and Delilah* was inspired by the story in the 16th chapter in the book of Judges in the Old Testament. The opera does not tell of Samson's rise to leadership nor the mighty feats he accomplished during that rise.[1] Instead, the composer, Camille Saint-Saëns, and his librettist cousin focused on the episode that led to Samson's (and the temple of Dagon's) downfall. The resounding theme of the opera emphasizes how a heroic man can be swayed and succumb to the wiles and charms of a beautiful, seductive woman. (So, what's new?)

For some unknown reason, Camille (with a man's name like Camille, you just have to be on a first-name basis) wrote the music for Act Two first. When Act Two was poorly received by a selected audience, he delayed further work on the opera for a few years. (Most audiences like to start with Act One.) Later a performance of Act One was similarly received. (But,

---

[1] One of these feats was to kill 1,000 Philistines with the jawbone of an ass. Probably hard to set this incident to music – and, probably it's even harder to stage.

of course, he was missing Act Two.) Despite these initial poor reviews of some of the opera's parts, Franz Listz accepted and conducted the opera's premiere some eight years after Camille received the libretto from his cousin. Even then it was another 13 years before the opera was performed in his home country of France.

ACT ONE

(Scene One): A public square in the city of Gaza. On one side of the square is the entrance to the temple of the Philistine god Dagon. In the square a crowd of Hebrews is voicing its dejection and hopelessness. They have been vanquished and enslaved by the cruel Philistines who now occupy their land. They feel their God, the true God, has abandoned them and they do not understand why. Samson comes out of the crowd and responds to their complaints. He tells them God has not abandoned them. God has heard their prayers and they will break from bondage. The crowd says Samson speaks vainly. They have no arms. They have no power. All they have is tears. Samson reminds them God is powerful — He brought their forefathers out of Egypt. The crowd replies God has stopped listening to their pleas. (In other words, what's He done for us lately?) Samson becomes irritated with their lack of faith and tells them God will endow them with power. His arguments finally convince the crowd. They say they will eliminate their fear and they will trust in God for their salvation.

(Scene Two): Abimelech, the satrap of Gaza, enters with a host of Philistine warriors and soldiers.[2] (Mean people rarely travel alone.) He's upset with the Hebrews for disturbing him with their pitiful outcries. He recognizes the natives are restless, but he says it will all come to naught. He says the Hebrews will always be a conquered people — there is no hope for them. (This talk should not be confused with a pep talk or a motivational speech.) He ridicules the God of the Hebrews by saying their God is deaf to their pains and powerless to

[2] A satrap is basically a second-level bureaucrat. It has nothing to do with golf or hunting.

act. He boasts that Dagon, the Philistine god, is above all gods — that Jehovah flees from Dagon like a dove from a vulture. (This is how the guy got to be satrap — he can make a nice little off-the-cuff metaphor, like this one.)

Samson takes great exception to Abimelech's words that defame God. He says this is the hour God will begin the overthrow of all these unrighteous, ungodly people. Samson definitely got the satrap's full attention. The satrap completely loses his composure and his temper. He grabs up a sword and attacks Samson. (A bad mistake — he should have had a course in anger management.) The armed Abimelech is no match for the unarmed Samson. Samson wrests the sword from him and mortally stabs him.[3] A gaggle of Philistine soldiers rushes to attack Samson, but he is able to brandish the sword and keep them at bay. In the confusion that follows, Samson and the crowd of Hebrews escape unharmed.

(Scene Three): The High Priest of Dagon (or, the High POD, for short) enters followed by all of his attendants and guards. (Mean people rarely travel alone — remember?) He looks down on the slain Abimelech's body (he does avoid stepping on him) and calls for vengeance against all the perpetrators. He tells the Philistine soldiers to fly after the slaves (this is the way people talked in those days — it has nothing to do with being airborne) and cut them down. Hmm, wait! — there seems to be a problem with the troops. One soldier says his limbs are heavy as if bound with chains. Another says he feels faint and is unable to draw his weapon. An angry High POD calls them all cowards (Sure — and why isn't this guy going after Samson?).

(Scene Four): A Philistine messenger enters and reports the situation with Samson and the Hebrews is getting worse. ("Samson and the Hebrews" — sounds like the name of a rock group.) He reports they are gaining more power and ravaging everything in their path. (Maybe they *are* a rock group.) This bit of news seems to be the final straw — the soldiers decide

[3] That means that Abimelech's singing is over for the evening - although he does take up floor space for a while.

to leave that village and return to their homes. (Dagon, Schmagon — we're outa here!) The High POD curses Samson, but he not only leaves with the men he called cowards, he's in front of them.

(Scene Five): Several old Hebrew men and women enter. They thank God they have been delivered from their enemy. They continue singing praises as Samson and the Hebrews enter.

(Scene Six): Delilah enters from the gates of Dagon's temple. She is followed by a number of Philistine women, who are the priestesses of Dagon. They bring garlands of flowers for the victorious Hebrew troops. (It seems like the Dagon followers want to be on the winning side.) Delilah has her eyes on Samson. She tells him to follow her and she will provide him sweet comfort. Samson is interested in what that sweet comfort might be, but realizes he is being tempted. He prays he can resist this beautiful woman. An Aged Hebrew Man sees and senses what is taking place. (That's why he's aged.) He states his alarm for Samson and for the Hebrews alike if Samson yields to Delilah's temptation.

The priestesses of Dagon begin a sensual dance. They wave their garlands of flowers and with voluptuous poses attempt to entice the Hebrew warriors. Delilah is the lead dancer and poser. She has her sights set on Samson. He makes a weak attempt to avoid looking at her, but he finds himself following her every move and gesture. Delilah continues to tempt Samson as she sings the charming *Printemps qui commence* (O Spring that is beginning) that thoroughly bewitches Samson. Samson's troubled expression says it all. The Aged Hebrew Man sees what is happening and prays Samson will not yield to this poisonous woman.

ACT TWO

(Scene One): An undisclosed time later, on the terrace of Delilah's dwelling in the valley of Sorek. The terrace is set within a garden that has beautiful tropical foliage. Delilah is seated on a bench by the door that leads to her dwelling. She is exquisitely dressed. She is reminiscing about her association with Samson. She sings the lovely aria, *Armour! Viens aider ma faiblesse* (O love! Come and help me in my weakness). She is making love to Samson in order to appease her god, Dagon, and to render Samson powerless. She believes he is under her domination, but she now appeals to Love to make him her total captive. Only if Samson is made captive will he lose his strength and allow her people to regain their power.

(Scene Two): The High POD enters the terrace. He complains to Delilah the Hebrews cannot be controlled because of Samson's feats (actually, it's not only his feats, but his hands and arms as well). He further complains Samson has caused his brave soldiers (obviously this is a misprint or a translation error) to flee. He thinks Delilah has lost her power over Samson. Delilah says something like "No way, Jose!" or maybe she said, "Not in the least, priest!" She boasts Samson may be mighty in battle, but he's a slave to her when they're together. This makes the High POD feel better. (Delilah seems to have a knack for making men feel better.) He wants to give her gold for Samson. Delilah scorns that offer. She says she hates Samson more than anyone — she says she will bring Samson down because of her hatred, not for gold. (Aha! Delilah has a flaw — she's not a good businesswoman.) Delilah tells the High POD she has tried three times to find out the secret of Samson's power, but Samson has resisted telling her.[4] She is sure the next time they meet he will confide his secret. She will use her surest weapons — her feigned grief and tears. (OK, guys — don't say you haven't been warned.) Together they sing their pep rally jingle...

"Let hatred in disguise now chain him!
Let love with gilded links enchain him!
May passion his reason enthrall,
That lowly his proud head may fall!"

Nice jingle — it accurately sums up their desire and their goal. The High POD leaves, encouraged by Delilah's devotion to their goal. After he leaves, Delilah has second thoughts about

---

[4] FYI, the three times: He was bound with (1) bowstrings, (2) new ropes, and (3) locks of hair.

what she told the High POD; she wonders if she really does own Samson.

(Scene Three): Samson enters the terrace, berating himself for being so weak he cannot stay away from Delilah. (Samson is a man of strong indecision.) Delilah greets him with false words of love and begins to execute her plan. She states her love, but feigns grief and weeping. She says Samson must not love her because he is withholding his heart and his secrets from her. The bewitched Samson states he loves her, but he would sin against God if he were to divulge the secret of his God-given power. Delilah sings of her unqualified love for him in the opera's best known number, *Mon coeur s'ouvre a ta voix* (My heart opens at your voice). Her words seem to ensnare Samson, but he still refuses to tell her his secret. Back and forth the dialogue between the two goes, neither giving into the other. Finally, Delilah tells Samson he has a loveless heart and she despises him. She tells him farewell and stalks into her house.

Poor overmatched Samson stands confused for a moment, but then in his weakness, he hastily follows her. After he leaves the terrace, some Philistine soldiers approach the house. In a few minutes Delilah appears and in a victorious voice calls for the soldiers to come quickly and take Samson captive. Samson's voice is heard plaintively saying, "I am betrayed!" as the soldiers rush into the house.

ACT THREE

(Scene One): The courtyard of the prison at Gaza. Samson is blinded, heavily chained, and shorn of hair. (A Philistine punster might call him the "Lock Less Monster.") He is yoked to a mill wheel that grinds grain. (He would like to go against the grain, but he's too weak.) He is forced to walk in a never-ending circle. Samson is repentant. He has sinned against God and he bemoans his sin and his punishment. He also feels the pain of betraying the Hebrew people who have been enslaved again with his imprisonment. A chorus of other Hebrew captives in the prison berates Samson for his weakness and his failure. Samson prays to God that the Hebrew people not be punished for his transgression. His prayers and work are interrupted when some Philistine soldiers enter the courtyard, unfasten him from the mill wheel, and escort him to the Temple of Dagon.

(Scene Two): The interior of the Temple of Dagon. The temple has a vaulted roof that is supported by two huge pillars. A sacrificial altar and a large statue of Dagon are on one side of the temple. The Dagon priests and priestesses are gathered on the other side.

Samson brought down the house

Already there is a large crowd in the temple even though it is early morning. The High POD is there amid the temple priestesses. Delilah enters followed by young women carrying wine cups. It is celebration time. The women dance and all drink to the festive occasion. The blinded Samson enters. He remains heavily chained and is guided by a child to emphasize his helplessness. The High POD and the "worshippers" taunt Samson and toast Delilah for her accomplishment. (Adding insult to injury.)

In an aside, the repentant Samson prays God will help him. Delilah approaches Samson and taunts him about their so-called love affair. She says her vengeance is complete for herself, her god, and her people. Samson doesn't speak to her, but continues to pray. The High POD now makes fun of Samson's powerless God. Samson now prays aloud for all to hear. He asks that his lost power be restored for just one moment. The crowd makes fun of Samson's pleas.

The High POD begins their formal celebration and worship of Dagon. (This probably means that the priests are taking up a collection.) While this ceremony is taking place, the contrite Samson remains in the centre of the scene praying. The crowd praises Dagon and gives him thanks for this great victory. Then the exuberant High POD tells Samson to fall on his knees before the huge statue of Dagon. He tells the child to lead Samson to a place where all can see and deride him. Samson tells the child to lead him to the pair of marble pillars that support the entire temple. Samson places himself between the pillars and asks God for one moment of power in order to show everyone the Hebrew God is the true God. His prayer is answered. Samson regains his strength long enough to topple the pillars. The temple falls amid the cries, screams, and death of all of its inhabitants.

And, now we have the answer to that old riddle...

"Who is the greatest actor in the Bible?"

The answer is Samson, because he brought down the house".

Yes — you're right — it's time to move on to another opera.

FIVE YEARS LATER
(A Fabricated and Unauthorized Epilogue)

– Samson, of course, died with all the others in the temple. His body was recovered and buried by relatives between Zorah and Eshtaol. (Those are places, not people.)

– The Aged Hebrew continues his regimen of jogging and exercise. He doesn't seem to age any more. Oh, yes, one of his ancestors is Methuselah — it must be in the genes.

– The child that led Samson to the temple's pillars escaped death because Samson told him to leave the temple ASAP. He remains in the Gaza area, working as a tourist guide.

– The crowd of Hebrews is still a crowd of Hebrews.

***

Il Trovatore

(The Troubador)
By Giuseppe Verdi
(1813-1901)
Libretto by Salvatore Cammarano
Based on a play by Antonio Garcia Gutierrez

MAIN CHARACTERS

Duchess Leonora, a lady-in-waiting	*Soprano*
Azucena, A Biscayan gypsy woman	*Mezzo-soprano*
Manrico, a Chieftain under the Prince of Biscay	*Tenor*
Count di Luna, a young Noble of Aragon	*Baritone*
Ferrando, Di Luna's Captain of the Guard	*Bass*
Inez, confidante of Leonora	*Soprano*
Ruiz, a soldier in Manrico's service	*Tenor*

Place: Aragon and Biscay, in Spain
Time: Mid Fifteenth Century
First Performance: Teatro Apollo, Rome, January 19, 1853
Original Language: Italian

Il Trovatore was one of three great operas Giuseppe Verdi composed within a three-year period. (The other two are *Rigoletto* and *La Traviata*.) Salvatore Cammarano was the librettist for *Il Trovatore* as well as for two lesser-known operas by Verdi (*La Battaglia di Legnano* and *Luisa Miller*.) [1]

Verdi, who composed 26 operas, is considered to be Italy's most famous composer. Verdi, commenting about his music, said he placed emotional sensibility above intellect in his operas. (Probably thinking about us operagoers.) In Verdi's biographical summary it's noted he founded a home for invalid musicians in Milan in 1898. (Don't get your retirement hopes up. It's not a home for bad (in-*vah*-led) musicians; it's a home for sickly (*in*-val-id) musicians.)

Verdi said about *Il Trovatore* that he thought he had done well, but if not, he had done it the way he felt it. History proves

[1] In addition, Cammarano was the librettist for two of Donizetti's operas, the more notable being *Luci di Lammermoor*.

Verdi did very well. Critics applaud the melodies in *Il Trovatore* but generally flog the plot, judging it to be too convoluted. Maybe it's because most of the real action doesn't happen within the acts — the performers just sing about it like a flash-back. Whatever.

Il Trovatore is about two brothers who don't know they're brothers, who are on different warring sides and who are rivals for the same girl. Included in the plot are a witch burned at the stake, a baby brutally murdered, some gypsies, some nuns, a singing knight, a suicide, a beheading, and lots of name-calling. Pretty normal makeup for an opera. What's this stuff about a convoluted plot?

ACT ONE (The Duel)

(Scene One): A hall in the palace of Aliaferia in Aragon. Adjoining the hall on one side is an entrance to Count di Luna's apartments. It is late at night. Ferrando and a group of servants are standing near the entrance. In the background there are armed men standing guard. Ferrando is telling the servants and guards to be alert. (After all, they're getting paid overtime.) Ferrando expects Count di Luna to return at any moment from his nightly courtship of Leonora. The Count fears he is losing his beloved Leonora to a troubadour, who has been serenading her. (The Count must not be able to sing as well.) The Count wants the troubadour apprehended. Ferrando's listeners could care less; they are sleepy. They would rather hear the story about the tragic death of the Count's brother that happened many years ago. Ferrando is happy to oblige. The servants and guards gather around Ferrando as he tells them the story.

It all happened when the Count's brother, Garzia, was a baby. An old witch was discovered by Garzia's crib and was driven away. (With a cudgel, not a car.) Shortly thereafter, the boy became ill, so everyone thought the witch had placed a curse on him. They tracked down the witch and had her burned at the stake. (Incidentally, that's the only way to get a witch hot and bothered.) As the story goes, the witch's daughter, a gypsy, got revenge. On the day of the witch's death, it is believed the gypsy daughter abducted Garzia and threw the infant in the same fire that consumed the gypsy's mother. (This doesn't seem like a feel-good or therapeutic story.) The remains of an infant boy were found in the ashes of that fire. The gypsy woman was never seen again. Garzia's father never believed his son was dead. On his deathbed, he told his other son, Count di Luna, to search for his brother Garzia. (Would the Count be searching for his no-Count brother?) Nothing much has happened since the witch was burned at the stake, although it is believed the spirit of the witch still haunts the castle to this very day. (Don't they know it's bad luck to be superstitious?)

As he finishes the story, a clock starts chiming midnight. What timing! The guards and servants are wide-awake now. They may not sleep for a day or two. They move away from Ferrando and return to their places of duty.

A little knight music?

(Scene Two): Meanwhile, in the palace garden by Leonora's apartments, Leonora and her close friend Inez are deep in conversation. Leonora is telling Inez she fell in love with a mysterious knight at a tournament some time ago. He won all of his bouts and she crowned him victor. (The winners always get the girls.) Then our hero disappeared for a while. But, now he has recently returned as a troubadour to serenade her below her window. (A little knight music?) She tells Inez he is her true love; she can never love another. She says without him she will die. (She probably will anyway, eventually.) Inez tells her friend she hopes her love will not be in vain. They walk up the stairs into Leonora's palace apartments.

Count di Luna enters, telling of his love for Leonora, as he begins to walk up the stairs to her apartment. However, he hears the notes of a lute and a man singing. It's obviously his rival, the troubadour, who is singing his love for Leonora. She has heard him also. She rushes down the stairs to embrace him. Well, heavy clouds have obscured the moon and the garden is rather dark. Leonora's vision is impaired by the darkness and she makes a little mistake — she embraces the Count. So, there she is, hugging the wrong guy, when the troubadour comes out of the shadows. He angrily reproaches her for being in the arms of another. Leonora quickly begs forgiveness for her mistake, telling the troubadour how much she loves him. The troubadour believes her. Unfortunately, so does Count di Luna. The Count demands to know his rival's name. The troubadour says his name is Manrico. The Count is even more furious than before. He denounces Manrico as an exile and a follower of the Prince of Biscay, his enemy. The two men trade insults back and forth. (They're both big on using names like Rogue and Coward.) Leonora pleads with them to stop. She tells the Count she will hate him forever if anything happens to Manrico. Neither man listens. They draw their swords and leave the garden to fight as Leonora falls senseless to the ground. (Some would say the two men are the senseless ones.)[2]

ACT TWO (The Gypsy)

(Scene One): It is dawn in the mountains in Biscay. There is a fire burning in the ruins of a hovel in the middle of a

---

[2] This is a trifle disappointing. Here we were about to have the first real action in the opera and what happens? The principals go offstage to fight.

gypsy encampment. It is many days after the confrontation in the garden between Count di Luna and Manrico.

As dawn breaks, the gypsies awake and begin their daily tasks. They take their places at their forges and we hear one of the most familiar operatic melodies as they work — *The Anvil Chorus*. The music emphasizes their work on the forges — they bring their hammers down on the metal forges in rhythm with the music. The men pause in their work for a wine break as they exalt the free and easy life of the gypsy. (It sure seems free and easy — it didn't take long for a wine break, did it?)

Seated by the fire in the hovel are Azucena and Manrico. Azucena follows *The Anvil Chorus* with the familiar aria *Stride la vampa* (The blaze is harsh). She sings of a poor gypsy woman who was burned at the stake and she cries out for vengeance. After she finishes, all of the gypsies leave to go forage for food in the city. (Maybe they're just getting away from the morose Azucena.) Only Azucena and Manrico remain.

Manrico is puzzled by Azucena's call for vengeance and asks for an explanation. She then tells him the woman burned at the stake was her mother, and she seeks revenge. She tells how she attempted to avenge her mother by abducting her enemy's child from his crib in order to burn him in the same fire that killed her mother. Alas! She threw a child in the fire only to discover it was her own son and not the baby she had abducted! What a horrific story! We're talking bizarre!

Manrico suddenly reasons Azucena may not be his mother after all. Azucena hastens to assure him he is her son. (She does her best to get the cat back into the bag.)[3]

She reminds him how she raised him. She reminds him how most recently she rescued him from the battlefield where he had been left for dead and then nourished him back to health. He acknowledges he was near death, wounded by the lance thrust of Count di Luna. She shakes her head in

---

[3] Of course, you astute readers have already deduced that Manrico was the abducted baby and is the brother of Count di Luna. Our apologies to everyone else if we spoiled the ending for you.

bewilderment at Manrico. She knows Manrico spared the life be of the Count in a duel when the Count was helpless. Manrico agrees. He says he doesn't know why, but as he was about to strike the mortal blow, his arm was held back and he heard a voice telling him to spare the Count. (Azucena is a little worried her son is hearing voices, but she doesn't say anything.) Azucena wants revenge. She pleads with him to kill Count di Luna the next time they meet.

A messenger interrupts their conversation with a two-part message from the Prince of Biscay. First, their troops have taken the Castellor fortress and Manrico is needed there at once. Second, there is a prevalent rumor of his death on the battlefield. The rumor is causing the broken-hearted Leonora to enter a convent within the day. Manrico cannot bear the thought of losing her. He immediately prepares to leave, ignoring Azucena's desperate pleas to stay. A hasty farewell and he is gone.

(Scene Two): In a cloister within the Convent of La Croix near the Castellor fortress. It is night. Count di Luna, Ferrando, and some of his retainers are hiding in the shadows.[4] The Count has come to take Leonora away from the convent by force before she takes her vows as a nun. The Count sings his familiar aria, *Il balen del suo sorriso* (The lightning of her smile) as he expresses his love for Leonora. Count di Luna tells his men to stay concealed until he gives the high sign. (Can a bad guy give a high sign, or would he have to give a low sign?)

A bell tolls, signaling the start of the ceremony of Leonora's renunciation. A chorus of nuns is heard proclaiming the solitude of their life and their obedience to God. Leonora and Inez enter, accompanied by a group of women attendants. Inez is sorrowful about being separated from her friend. Leonora comforts her as she prepares to join the nuns.

Count di Luna and his men come out of hiding. The Count announces he has come to take Leonora away. The sur-

---

[4] These retainers are not the Count's orthodontic devices for straightening his teeth; they are just his servants and employees.

prised and frightened Leonora says he has no right. Before anyone else can speak or act, Manrico bursts upon the scene. Leonora and the Count are shocked to see one they thought dead to be very much alive. Leonora rushes into his arms, hardly believing he is real. The Count and Manrico resume their tirade of insults for each other (e.g., I never liked you and I never will). Ferrando warns Manrico to leave immediately and not tempt fate. Manrico does not have to worry about tempting fate. Ruiz, an officer in Manrico's command, enters with a large contingent of soldiers. (Now all of Leonora's acquaintances who weren't invited are at the convent.) The outnumbered Count di Luna, Ferrando, and their retainers (servants — remember?) find it easy to leave without accomplishing their mission.

In the closing chorus, Manrico and Leonora sing, "The two of us be united!" The Count and Ferrando sing, "The two of them be cursed!" And, the nuns sing, "The two of them be blessed!" (Most of life depends on your point of view.)

ACT THREE (The Gypsy's Son)

(Scene One): Count di Luna's military encampment outside the Castellor fortress. At the right is the Count's tent. In the background the fortress may be seen. Sentries are everywhere; groups of soldiers are in tents scattered around the encampment. (The Count's intention is to have his soldiers in tents but not intense — hopefully, this is not confusing.) It is several days after the confrontation at the Convent of La Croix.

Ferrando comes out of the Count's tent and gives a pep talk to the troops. He says the siege will soon be over: Tomorrow the battle will begin and victory will most assuredly be theirs. The soldiers respond with the stirring *Soldiers' Chorus*. The Count comes out of his tent. He glances toward the fortress, bitterly lamenting not only the loss of Leonora, but also the realization his sworn enemy has her in his arms.

Ferrando interrupts the Count's thoughts by bringing a captive before him. He tells the Count the captive is a gypsy woman who was lurking near their camp and who is suspected of spying. The suspected spy is Azucena. When asked, she tells the Count her name and where she is from. Her demeanor and her answers to their probing questions give her terrible secret away. Ferrando identifies her as the gypsy who abducted the baby 20 years ago. In her anguish, she calls for her son, Manrico, to save her. Count di Luna exults at his good fortune — he not only has his brother's murderer, he also has his hated rival's mother at his mercy. In a rousing chorus, Azucena says God will strike the Count dead for his injustices, the Count condemns Azucena to death, and Ferrando and the soldiers consign her to Hell. (Again, some different points of view.)

(Scene Two): A hall in the fortress of Castellor. At the end of the hall is a balcony from which Count di Luna's enemy encampment can be seen. Manrico and Leonora are talking about their love for each other and their plan to marry that day. However, their wedding day may have to wait as they hear the call to arms from their enemy's camp. Then, some more bad news. Ruiz rushes in to tell Manrico the enemy is leading a gypsy woman in chains to a large pyre by their encampment. Manrico looks where Ruiz is pointing. He sees Azucena being placed on a pyre. He is horrified. He tells Leonora in halting speech the gypsy woman is his mother. He orders Ruiz to prepare his men for battle. As Ruiz leaves, Manrico sings the familiar aria, *Di quella pira* (Of that horrible pyre), declaring he cannot forsake his mother and he will save her or die. (He sings while Mom burns.) Ruiz returns with soldiers ready for battle. (These guys sure got ready fast.) They pledge themselves to follow their leader to rescue his mother. All leave as a distraught Leonora slumps to the floor. (For Leonora's part, one has to be a good slumper and fainter.)

ACT FOUR (The Torture)

(Scene One): A battlement of the Aliaferia palace in Aragon. On one side rising above the battlement there is a prison tower with barred windows. It is night and some time after the conflict at the Castellor Fortress. (Again, the audience never sees the conflict: The performers just refer to it.)

Ruiz has led Leonora to this place by the prison tower. She is heavily cloaked in an effort to conceal her identity. She has come to see if she can rescue Manrico. First, however, she has to bring the audience up-to-date.

Manrico and his men were defeated in their attempt to rescue Manrico's mother. Manrico was taken captive and is a prisoner with his mother in the prison tower. The Castellor Fortress also fell to Count di Luna and his troops. Leonora, Ruiz, and a few others were lucky to escape. Now, she is risking her life to see if there is a way to save Manrico.

She sings of her love for Manrico. In the background a chorus is heard chanting the beautiful *Miserere* for an approaching death. She then sings how broken-hearted and afraid she is. Manrico hears and responds with words that lament the slowness of death. He bids farewell to Leonora. She moves back into the shadows as she hears someone coming. (Someone must have heard the back-and-forth singing.)

Count di Luna and some of his men enter. He indicates to them the place where the execution of the prisoners is to take place. The mother is to be burned at the stake; the son is to be beheaded. (Manrico would like to be beheaded all right — be headed home.) The men leave as the Count wonders out loud where Leonora is. Wonder no longer — Leonora comes out of the shadows and confronts him. She begs and pleas for Manrico's life over and over again. The Count will have none of it. Each plea is met with his anger. He tells her, "The greater your tenderness, the greater my pleasure when I think of his excruciating death." (Nice fellow.) Finally, she tells him she will be his if he would but spare Manrico. She would just like a few moments with Manrico first. She has made the Count an offer he can't refuse. He accepts her proposal and his anger turns to joy. They leave to enter the prison tower together. What the Count has not seen nor heard, however, is Leonora swallowing some poison from her ring and saying, "He shall have but a corpse!"

(Scene Two): The prison cell of Manrico and Azucena. It is dimly lit by a small lamp from the vaulted ceiling. There are two pallets where mother and son are seated. Up high is the only window and it is barred.

Mother and son are comforting each other. Azucena relives her mother's death and is terrified about dying at the stake. Manrico is able to calm her as they sing a mournful but beautiful duet *Ai nostri monti* (Home to our mountains). Azucena goes to sleep.

Without warning, the prison door opens and Leonora enters. Manrico thinks he's dreaming at first, but not after he receives a long, warm embrace. She tells him to hasten, to leave quickly. He is more than willing, but balks when Leonora says she must stay. He quickly surmises she has given herself to Count di Luna for his life. His love turns to hatred. He says his life is worth nothing. He calls her a wretch who sold her love. The poison starts to take effect earlier than Leonora had anticipated. She can no longer stand, and collapses (another diva dive) at Manrico's feet. She tells him what she has done. She says she never would have betrayed their love. He realizes what a fool he has been. He takes her in his arms and tries to both apologize and comfort her in her last few minutes of life.

Count di Luna enters with some soldiers. He is irate when he sees how Leonora tricked him and escaped him again (permanently this time). He orders the soldiers to take Manrico and execute him at once. The soldiers roughly take Manrico away as he cries out he will shortly join Leonora in Heaven. (If you're beheaded, you will be there shorter, if not shortly.) The commotion causes Azucena to awaken. She calls out for her son, not realizing he is not there. The Count triumphantly tells her he is dying on the scaffold. The drum rolls announce the sentence has been carried out. Azucena with deep sarcasm turns to the Count and tells him her mother has been avenged at last. In scathing words she tells him the man you just beheaded was your brother. The Count is horrified when he learns the truth.

FIVE YEARS LATER
(A Fabricated and Unauthorized Epilogue)

- Azucena, unfortunately, was burned at the stake right after Manrico was beheaded. Just because the Count made a little mistake with his brother didn't mean he would spare Azucena.

- Count di Luna has no regrets regarding his brother. He did resign his commission to enjoy his inherited wealth. He has mellowed a little. He still favors capital punishment as long as it's not too harsh.

- Ferrando, the Count's right-hand man, also resigned his commission when he was passed over for the Duke's old job. He is an executive for Ready Retainers, which supplies part-time and temporary help to businesses (including a little dentistry on the side).

- Inez married Ruiz. They live in Biscay with their children: Onez, Twoz, and Threez. Rumor has it that their fourth child will be named Lastz. (Not to be demeaning, but isn't that the name of a dog movie star?)

***

Aida

By Giuseppe Verdi
(1813-1901)
Libretto by Antonio Ghislanzoni
Based on a sketch by Mariette Bey

MAIN CHARACTERS

Aida, an Ethiopian girl and slave to Amneris	*Soprano*
Amneris, daughter of the Pharaoh	*Mezzo-soprano*
Amonasro, King of Ethiopia and father of Aida	*Baritone*
Pharaoh, King of Egypt	*Bass*
Radames, an Egyptian Captain of Pharaoh's army	*Tenor*
Ramfis, a high priest of Isis	*Bass*
Messenger	*Tenor*

Place: Memphis and Thebes
Time: Ancient Egypt during the reign of the Pharaohs
First Performance: Cairo Opera House; Cairo, Egypt;
December 24, 1871
Original Language: Italian

Aida is an opera about Egypt and a couple of Ethiopians composed by an Italian and sung in Italian. With this diversity, it figures that its premiere was in an Italian opera house located in Cairo, Egypt. The premiere was an enormous success for its composer, Giuseppe Verdi, who was nearing age 60 when he wrote it. Some believe Verdi named the opera *Aida* because he was an avid crossword-puzzle enthusiast and wanted to introduce a new four-letter word. The opera could easily have been titled *Radames,* because it's a story of how a victorious Egyptian army commander gave up Egypt's throne for his love of an enslaved Ethiopian princess. (When it comes to romance, army commanders do not always make the right decision.)

ACT ONE

(Scene One): The great hall of Pharaoh's palace in Memphis (Egypt, not Tennessee). In the background, temples and pyramids can be seen through a large gate of the palace. Radames, the captain of the guard, converses with Ramfis, the high priest of Isis, who tells Radames the Ethiopians are threatening Egypt in the Nile Valley – perhaps a forerunner of the song *Trouble (in River City)* from *The Music Man* – and Egypt will have to send an army to resist them. Ramfis says Isis has named the person (she has instructed Ramfis to be politically correct) to lead the Egyptian force. With a knowing wink and a nod to Radames, he leaves to go counsel the Pharaoh.

Radames is excited at the prospect of leading Egypt's army and returning as conqueror to woo Aida, the beautiful Ethiopian slave girl with whom he is secretly in love. He expresses his thoughts in the familiar aria *Celeste Aida* (Radiant Aida). Unfortunately, Aida is the slave of Amneris, the Pharaoh's daughter, who has her royal eyes on Radames. Amneris enters and speaks with Radames. With her feminine intuition working overtime, she fears she has a rival. (She's right.) Meanwhile, Radames, in an aside, worries he has let the cat out of the bag.

Aida enters and Amneris's jealousy and suspicions are even more apparent. Aida is noticeably sad and says the talk of war upsets her. Actually, she is concerned about her native country, Ethiopia. Her captors do not know she is the daughter of Amonasro, the King of Ethiopia. While Aida fears, Radames frets and Amneris fumes. (It's easy for Amneris to fume because she has the hots for Radames, which in Egypt's climate is not difficult at all.)

Pharaoh enters to a fanfare of trumpets, preceded by his guards and followed by Ramfis, ministers, dignitaries, priests, priestesses, officers, soldiers, a few stagehands and a couple of ushers.[1] A messenger confirms that the Ethiopians have invaded Egypt and are marching on Thebes. (Thebes is a city in Egypt. It is not the name of an Ethiopian athletic shoe.) He also says the Ethiopians are being led by Amonasro, their king (and unknown to all the Egyptians, Aida's father – remember?). While the throng roars in anger and Aida cries out in fear, the Pharaoh tells Radames Isis has decreed that he will lead Egypt's troops and he must go to the temple to be vested with sacred armor. The throng roars its approval and all leave

[1] Some believe Pharaoh is the ruler because he's the straightest man in Egypt.

except for Aida, who remains in the hall, mournfully torn between the love for her father, her country and Radames. A tough spot to be in – and it's only the end of the first scene.

A veil? Where's that sacred armour the Pharaoh promised me?

(Scene Two): The interior of the Temple of Vulcan at Memphis. In the center of the temple is an altar; along each side are various symbols and statues of Egyptian deities. Ramfis, his priests and priestesses are gathered around the altar, where clouds of incense rise from tripods nearby. In fact, the whole temple is incensed – these guys are angry! The priests chant and the priestesses dance, showing their devotion to their local god, Phtha. (Also spelled Ptah and Phthah; why didn't someone buy a vowel?)

The unarmed Radames enters and proceeds to the altar. At the altar, Ramfis gives Radames the temple's sacred sword and a silver veil for his head. (Radames is probably thinking, "A veil? Where's that sacred armor the Pharaoh promised me?") Ramfis offers a prayer to Phtha for the protection of Egypt. After Ramfis gives Radames the correct pronunciation of Phtha, Radames repeats the prayer and everybody joins in the chorus, concluding this dramatic incantation.

ACT TWO

(Scene One): The palace apartments of Amneris. An undisclosed number of days have passed. Word has reached the palace – no doubt spread by Radames himself – that Radames and his army have been victorious. The slaves of Amneris are preparing her for the victory parade, and she is in a festive mood as they dance and sing of the delights of love that await her. (Her slaves may be good dancers and singers, but they are poor prognosticators.)

Aida enters and Amneris, feigning kindness, deceitfully tells her Radames has been killed in action. Aida's grief confirms her suspicions and Amneris admits she lied just to trap Aida, and that Radames is really alive! Aida's grief turns to joy, but now her boss knows her secret. When Amneris threatens her with cruel punishment and humiliation, Aida almost reveals her royal origin (although she's really thinking of filing a grievance with the Personnel Department). Instead, Aida begs for forgiveness as she confesses her secret love. Amneris generously accepts none of Aida's pleas and exits, to the sounds of triumph and celebration.

(Scene Two): An entrance to the city leading to the Temple of Ammon. On a platform overlooking the scene are two large thrones that have been set up for the Pharaoh and his daughter. The scene is crowded with people, which is evidently a union requirement. The Pharaoh enters through a triumphal arch with his large retinue and ascends to the throne. [2] The scene becomes even more crowded as Amneris enters with her smaller retinue, which includes Aida, and she takes her place on the throne by her father.

The crowd begins the victory celebration by singing *Gloria all'Egitto!* (Glory to Egypt!). Then, the very familiar *Grand March* music is heard as the victorious Egyptian troops enter

---

[2] A retinue means attendants. It is not a reference to the Pharaoh's anatomy. Actually, it's the same crowd of hangers-on that followed him in the last time he entered.

in a stately procession with their banners, chariots, spears, swords and the requisite statues of gods (evidently a requirement of the theological union). The procession ends as Radames rides up in his chariot for his hero's welcome. Amneris proudly crowns Radames with the victor's laurel.

Radames orders the Ethiopian captives, in chains, brought forth for their judgment. Among them is Aida's father, Amonasro, disguised as a mere officer (and a gentleman, we presume). Aida recognizes her father and surprises everybody by embracing him, but he warns her not to reveal his true identity as king.

The Pharaoh must now decide the punishment of the captives. Naturally, Amonasro, Aida, the other captives and the slaves ask the Pharaoh for mercy. Naturally, Ramfis and the priests demand their deaths. Pharaoh mourns that he must follow the will of the gods, but Radames intercedes and asks him to grant their freedom as his reward. Ramfis consents, but only if Aida and Amonasro remain as hostages in Egypt. The Pharaoh agrees. He then declares Radames will be his successor and be rewarded by having the hand of his daughter. (Actually, his reward will be all of her.) The triumphal chorus *Gloria all'Egitto!* is repeated, with only Radames and Aida expressing their sorrow. Amonasro isn't too pleased, either.

ACT THREE

The banks of the River Nile, with the Temple of Isis in the background. Palm trees line the banks of the river. It is a bright, moonlit night. Sounds of chanting come from the temple. (Some of the priests got their jobs purely by chants.)

Amneris and Ramfis arrive by boat and enter into the temple, where she is to pray and receive a blessing before her wedding. Aida enters, heavily veiled, mourning that she will never see her homeland again. (Maybe she needs a thinner veil.) She expresses her longing for Ethiopia in the aria *O, patria mia, mai piu ti rivedro* (Oh, native land, I ne'er shall see thee more).

Her father, Amonasro, enters and recognizes Aida right away, despite her veil. He berates Aida for her love of Radames, because Radames is her country's conqueror and enemy. He tells her a new uprising is planned and she must help her country by finding out the proposed route of the Egyptian army. Aida is reluctant at first but the promise of returning to Ethiopia with Radames at her side is compelling. She finally yields to his demands. Amonasro, in the manner befitting a disguised king, then hides behind some palm trees as Radames approaches. Radames is overjoyed in seeing Aida – but, knowing he is spoken for, she gives him the cold shoulder (remember the climate in Egypt? – this was not easy).

Radames convinces Aida of his love for her and only her. (Have you noticed Aida is easily swayed?) They decide escape to Ethiopia is their only choice. Radames says he knows a route through a pass that will be safe until morning. After that, the Egyptian army will guard it to ambush the Ethiopians. Remembering her father's orders, Aida asks him the name of the pass, and Radames tells her it is the Pass of Napata. Immediately Amonasro springs from his hiding place, shouting the musical equivalent of a "Gotcha!" He reveals his true identity as king and says he will order his armies there at once. (Obviously Amonasro has some unrevealed, secret means of communication.)

Radames realizes he has unwittingly become a traitor for Aida's sake. Amonasro and Aida tell him he is guiltless and that it's fate and not his fault. They implore him to escape with them. At that moment, Amneris, shouting, "Traitor!" comes zooming out of the temple. Ramfis, priests, and the temple guards closely follow her. Evidently Amneris has been eavesdropping, not praying. Amonasro attempts to stab Amneris but Radames restrains him. Amonasro and Aida make their escape, pursued by the temple guards. Radames sees the hieroglyphics on the wall and surrenders, handing his sword (the sacred sword, remember?) to Ramfis.

ACT FOUR

(Scene One): A hall in Pharaoh's Palace. An entrance to the subterranean hall of judgment is on the left. A passageway to the prison of Radames is on the right.

A dejected Amneris stands alone in the hall, with conflicting emotions. She still loves Radames, but hates the fact that he was going to flee with Aida. She has the prison guards bring Radames before her. She offers to obtain a pardon for him if he will confess his guilt and renounce Aida. Radames refuses.[3] He says he still loves Aida. He blames Amneris for losing Aida and says he is ready to die. She begs him to reconsider, but Radames is resolute. She sadly dismisses him to be judged.

The guards escort Radames to the subterranean hall of judgment where the priests are waiting to try him. (Actually, the priests are very trying.) The priests ask Radames to defend himself, but he never responds to their accusations. (Maybe he really is hard of hearing.) In the meantime, Amneris is imploring the gods for mercy, but her prayer is not answered. Radames is found guilty and sentenced to be buried alive. (Radames would really like a second opinion.) The priests rejoice that justice has been done – they are a no-nonsense group. Amneris curses the priests for their cruelty and lack of mercy.

(Scene Two): The Temple of Vulcan, divided into two floors. The upper floor is the interior of the temple flooded with light. The lower floor is a large, darkened subterranean tomb with steps that lead up to a small opening in the upper floor.

Radames sits on the tomb steps as two priests on the upper floor put the last stone slab in place that covers the tomb. He sighs that he will never see his love, Aida, again. Suddenly Aida, without her veil, moves toward him out of the shadows – she has willingly entered the tomb to die with her lover. Radames, having been taught to leave no stone unturned, vainly attempts to dislodge the stone slab that entombs them. When he fails, they realize their fate is sealed – and the tomb along with it. They embrace, singing of their love and bidding farewell to their time on earth in the stirring duet, *O, terra, addio!* (O, Earth, farewell!).

---

[3] In an early version of this work, Radames' first response was to say, "Pardon me?" This seemed to indicate Radames was hard of hearing and thus was edited out of the final version.

Above, on the upper floor of the temple, the priestesses dance and sing a death chant. Amneris enters wearing mourning robes. She flings herself on the entombment slab while she sobs a prayer to Isis that the soul of Radames will rest in peace. No doubt her prayer would be different if she had known Radames is with Aida at that moment. (And, vastly different if she knew about the epilogue!)

FIVE YEARS LATER
(A Fabricated and Unauthorized Epilogue)

- Contrary to popular belief, Aida and Radames did not die in the tomb. Aida knew of a secret tunnel that allowed them to escape unharmed and undetected. They made their way to the Cyclades in the Aegean Sea, where they have a prosperous business making marble figures and statues. They don't miss the heat of Egypt.

- Amneris continues to live the life of luxury. She mourned Radames all of six weeks before she married Radames' younger brother Ladames.

- The Pharaoh is busy overseeing the building of his personal pyramid. Also, he is strongly considering changing worship of the local god Phtha to Ma'at, goddess of truth, justice, and harmony. He believes his constituents need a heavy dose of her three specialties.

- The Pharaoh blamed Ramfis, the high priest, for the lack of support from Isis and Phtha while Egypt battled Ethiopia. Consequently, Ramfis was buried alive in the same tomb where Radames was buried. Unfortunately, Ramfis didn't find the secret tunnel.

- The priests and priestesses of Phtha are working hard on some new ceremonial rites instituted by their new high priest, Dorfus. After what happened to Ramfis, Dorfus is not leaving anything to chants.

- Amneris sent her slaves to work on Pharaoh's pyramid. She blamed them for her losing Radames.

- Amonasro, king of Ethiopia, disguised himself again. No one knows where he is (or who he is, for that matter).
***

Otello

(Othello)
by Giuseppe Verdi
(1813-1901)
Libretto by Arrigo Boito
Based upon Shakespeare's tragedy *Othello*

MAIN CHARACTERS

Othello, Governor of Cyprus	*Tenor*
Desdemona, Otello's wife	*Soprano*
Cassio, Otello's captain	*Tenor*
Iago, Otello's ensign	*Baritone*
Emilia, Iago's wife	*Mezzo-soprano*
Roderigo, a Venetian gentleman	*Tenor*
Montano, Otello's predecessor as governor of Cyprus	*Bass*
Lodovico, Ambassador of the Venetian Republic	*Bass*
A Herald	*Baritone*

Place: A seaport on Cyprus. Time: Late Fifteenth Century
First Performance: La Scala, Milan, Italy February 5, 1887
Original Language: Italian

Giuseppe Verdi began work on *Otello* in his late 60s and completed its composition when he was 74. He spent more time on its composition than any of his many other operas with the exception of *King Lear*. (After all, Shakespeare is a little difficult to read.) Verdi threatened to withdraw *Otello* if its premiere was unsuccessful, but he had nothing to worry about. The critics and audience of that day immediately accepted *Otello* as an opera of great importance — and so it has remained ever since. Verdi's *Otello* replaced Rossini's *Otello*, which had occupied a place of prominence for most of the 19th century. (Incidentally, the 'h' in Shakespeare's English-language *Othello* is removed in Verdi's Italian-language *Otello* — Othello is used in the text that follows.)

The opera *Otello* is the tragic story of a gullible and violently jealous husband who allowed the counsel of a cunning liar to destroy his marriage and his life. (As the story

-138-

unfolds, it seems a hanky causes this nosey husband to blow his good life.)

ACT ONE

A square in a harbor area overlooking the sea. On one side of the square is a tavern that has an adjoining arbor. Near-by is Othello's castle.

A crowd of Cypriots has gathered at the harbor anxiously awaiting the arrival of Othello's ship.[1] Othello is their general and governor who is returning from battle with the Turks. The crowd grows fearful for Othello's safety as a vicious storm is in progress. They see Othello's ship being tossed violently about. They see his ship's mainsail break and its prow crash on the reef. They are terrified and pray to God for the safety of the ship's occupants. Not to worry. Othello and his men are able to make it safely off the reef to shore. (In fact, they didn't even get wet.) Othello enters and lustily tells the ad-miring group about his great victory over the Turks. After the hurrahs die down, Othello leaves the scene to enter his nearby castle accompanied by some of his staff, soldiers, and sailors.

Well, not every one in the remaining crowd is admiring or happy. Roderigo, a Venetian gentleman, loves Othello's wife, Desdemona. (Obviously the rascal is a gentleman by title only.) Roderigo is sorry Othello's call to war didn't result in Desdemona becoming a widow. (And, with her looks, she would make a very becoming widow.) And, Iago (pronounced Yah-go), supposedly a loyal and trusted friend of Othello, expresses his contempt of Othello. Iago knows Roderigo des-ires Desdemona; so he tells Roderigo to be patient and follow his advice — he swears the lady will soon be his. Iago despises Othello because Othello promoted his hated rival Cassio to be captain in his stead. Iago wants to punish Othello and Cassio.

The homecoming victory celebration continues around a bonfire and the nearby tavern. Drinks are flowing freely and the devious Iago tells Roderigo to help him get Cassio drunk.

[1] Citizens of Cyprus are called Cypriots. To call them Cyprians would be calling them prostitutes. Look it up.

They start with a brindisi. (Brindisi is not a drink, but a drinking song.) Cassio actively participates in the brindisi although he has a hard time keeping up with the others. No wonder. They keep offering toasts and filling Cassio's glass until finally he gets drunk. After all these drinks he is toasted. Unfortunately Cassio has made a little mistake. He forgot he is supposed to be on guard duty that night.

Montano, the former governor of Cyprus, arrives to escort Cassio to his place of duty within the castle. Montano is appalled to see a drunken captain, although Cassio staggers forward as if to go to his place of duty. The always helpful Iago tells Montano that Cassio is like this every night. Roderigo, on the advice of Iago, laughs at Cassio's drunken condition. His laughter provokes the hot-tempered Cassio to lunge at him. Montano separates the two of them, but Cassio takes exception to his interference and now thinks Montano has insulted him. Cassio and Montano draw swords and begin dueling. Iago tells Roderigo to run around the harbor yelling "riot" to cause as much confusion as possible. Then, Iago acts like he is trying to stop the two dueling men. However, the duel continues until Othello enters and orders the two men to stop. Othello asks his "trusted" friend Iago to tell what happened. Iago says he doesn't know — they were all enjoying themselves and suddenly they began fighting as if they were bewitched. Iago says, " I'd rather both of my legs had been cut off rather than witness such a sight!" (But, then, Iago wouldn't have a leg to stand on.) [2] Othello is very angry, especially after he finds out Montano has been wounded. Montano had better practice or stay out of fights; after all, Cassio was drunk. Desdemona enters; evidently the com- motion has awakened her. (One wonders why she wasn't at the harbor to greet Othello when he first arrived.) Othello reprimands Cassio; he tells him he is no longer his captain. He orders Iago to take the soldiers, restore peace in the city, and help Montano in any way possible. (If Iago will just take the soldiers

[2] Iago is probably the same guy who said, "I'd give my right arm to be ambidextrous."

out of the tavern that will probably automatically restore peace in the city.) Iago leaves, secretly congratulating himself on this triumph over Cassio.

All leave the scene except for Othello and Desdemona. Othello is nice. He doesn't ask Desdemona why she wasn't at the harbor to greet him when he came home from battle. Instead, he tells her he loves her and she replies she loves him. They both sing of their love for each other and how lonely it was when they were apart. They pray their love will be forever and they embrace. This is all part of a beautiful love duet that some believe is one of the most beautiful love songs in all of opera. He kisses her three times, *Un bacio ... un bacio ... un altro bacio* (A kiss ... a kiss ... another kiss). They move slowly toward their castle, clasped in each other's arms. (Unfortunately for them the opera ain't over.)

ACT TWO
A room on the ground floor within Othello's castle. In the rear of the room there is an open doorway leading out to a garden. Iago and Cassio are having a conversation near the garden doorway. Iago convinces Cassio he should ask Desdemona to intercede with Othello in order to get his captaincy back. He tells Cassio to meet her in the nearby garden when she goes for her daily stroll. Sure enough, on schedule, Desdemona enters the garden accompanied by Emilia, Iago's wife. Cassio goes to meet them and to talk with Desdemona.

As they converse, Iago begins talking to himself about himself. He seems to relish being evil. He sings his famous soliloquy, *The Credo*: *Credo in un Dio crudel che m'ha creato simile a se* (I believe in a cruel God, who has fashioned me in his own image) He believes he was created evil by an evil god, and all the evil he does has already been pre- determined. In addition, he believes all men are either evil or buffoons. (Some believe this part of the text was written and inserted by the librettist's wife.)

Othello enters the room and approaches Iago. Iago pretends not to see him and mutters to himself so Othello can hear, "I don't like what I see at all." Othello glances out to the garden and sees Desdemona leaving with someone. Iago's words have the desired effect. Othello becomes suspicious and asks if the man who is with his wife is Cassio. Iago does not respond. Othello continues to question him. Iago answers in riddles and makes insinuations about Desdemona and Cassio that arouses Othello's jealousy. Iago feeds Othello's jealousy further by telling him to be on his guard.

Desdemona reappears in the garden accompanied by children, sailors and some island people. They sing to her and bring her flowers and other gifts. It is a beautiful scene that emphasizes the goodness of Desdemona. Othello is deeply moved and for a few minutes forgets his suspicions.

After the singing and gifting ends, Desdemona enters the hall followed by Emilia. She approaches Othello and immediately begins to ask Othello to pardon Cassio. Cassio is now a bad word to Othello. An irritated Othello asks if it was Cassio he saw her with in the garden. She allowed it was he and he was so grieved it touched her heart. She begs Othello to pardon him and restore his captaincy. The longer she talks about Cassio the angrier Othello gets. A very angry Othello finally says his head hurts (it's all in his mind) and he does not wish to discuss Cassio now. She attempts to soothe his head with her handkerchief (What? No Tylenol?). He throws her hanky on the ground and tells her to go away. She is puzzled and distraught about her husband's behavior and tries to make amends, but the jealous and angry Othello tells her to leave without giving her an explanation. (What we have here is a failure to communicate.) In the meantime, Emilia has picked up the discarded hanky. Iago wrestles the hanky away from Emilia, who realizes Iago is up to no good. It's not like Iago to arm wrestle over a hanky. Desdemona and Emilia leave, but not before Iago has warned Emilia to say nothing about the hanky.

Othello cries out in his anguish that he is living in a nightmare. His suspicions are even more terrible than any battle injuries. He seizes Iago by the throat and demands proof of Desdemona's unfaithfulness. Iago finds it a little difficult to speak until Othello releases his grip. He tells Othello he is resigning his commission because it is not safe for him to be sincere and loyal — he makes a pretense of leaving. Othello stops him from leaving. He doesn't know what to believe now. Is Desdemona faithful or not? Is Iago a loyal friend or not? He wants positive proof, one way or the other. (Normally the proof is in the pudding, but in this case there's no pudding.) Iago, sore throat and all, continues to weave his web of lies. He tells Othello that one night he overheard the sleeping Cassio in the midst of an obviously passionate dream call out to Desdemona that they should hide their love. (Othello doesn't think to ask Iago what he's doing in Cassio's sleeping quarters.) Iago embellishes his lie with other comments that Cassio supposedly says in his dream which, of course, angers Othello. Then, Iago tells Othello as proof of Desdemona's unfaithfulness he describes a handkerchief Cassio has in his possession that he believes is Desdemona's. Iago has just described the handkerchief Othello had given Desdemona as a token of his love. Iago is implying hankypanky. Othello is beside himself with anger; he wishes Cassio had a thousand lives because one life is not enough to satisfy his fury. Othello makes a solemn oath to heaven that he will exact his vengeance — and, the devious Iago, continues his charade as Othello's friend by making the same pledge.

ACT THREE

The great hall of Othello's castle. The great hall is richly and ornately furnished. On one side there is a raised throne. On the other side is a large portico. In the rear there is a terrace. It's a short time after Iago first convinced Othello there is some hanky-panky going on.

Othello and Iago are in the great hall, deep in conversation again, when they are interrupted by a Herald on the portico.

The Herald tells Othello a ship will arrive soon that is bringing the Ambassador of the Venetian Republic. Othello acknowledges the news, but he is really only interested in what Iago is telling him about Cassio and his wife. Iago tells Othello he will bring Cassio to this room and get him to gossip. If Othello will hide nearby and listen carefully, then Cassio will probably condemn himself. Othello is more than happy to agree; he is anxious to find out the truth. (Unfortunately, if he wants truth he should stay away from Iago.)

Desdemona enters as Iago goes to get Cassio. Desdemona's greeting is warm; Othello's response is cool. Desdemona innocently brings Cassio's name up again as she wishes to intercede for him. Othello gets another quick headache and asks her to bind his head with a handkerchief (Still no Tylenol?). She complies, but she doesn't use the hanky Othello wants to see. He tells her to fetch his gift hanky at once. She thinks it is a ploy to avoid talking about Cassio and, in saying so, she angers Othello even more. He accuses her of unfaithfulness and a puzzled and distraught Desdemona does not understand what has happened to their relationship. (Remember how lovey-dovey they were only a short time ago?) Othello grabs Desdemona roughly and pushes her out of the room. Alone, he cries out aloud about his complete state of dejection.

Iago returns and tells Othello to hide because Cassio will be there shortly. Cassio enters as Othello hides nearby. Iago cleverly engages Cassio in a conversation about Bianca, Cassio's mistress, such that the listening Othello thinks they are talking about Cassio having an affair with Desdemona. Cassio is puzzled about an embroidered handkerchief left in his bedroom and shows it to Iago. Othello does not hear this part of the conversation. He sees the hanky and immediately recognizes it as the one he gave to Desdemona. To Othello the hanky is the final proof of Desdemona's unfaithfulness and Cassio's betrayal. (To Othello, the hanky proves panky — the hanky is the "smoking gun".)

A trumpet fanfare followed by a cannon shot interrupts the conversation. The ship bringing the Venetian Ambassador has dropped anchor. Cassio leaves. Othello is ready for action. He approaches Iago and asks him to get some poison for his

To Othello, the hanky proves panky

wife, but Iago has a different idea. He suggests she be strangled in the bed she defiled. Othello says he likes Iago's sense of justice, but what of Cassio? Iago says he will take care of Cassio. Othello rewards Iago by making him his captain. Iago's plans couldn't be working any better. Their private conversation ends as the visiting ambassador and his retinue enter the great hall.

As the visitors enter the great hall, a chorus of voices is heard singing *The Lion of San Marco* in order to praise Othello. The visiting Venetian Ambassador, Lodovico, and his dignitaries are met by the home team of Othello, Roderigo, Iago, Desdemona, Emilia, and Othello's cadre of soldiers and officers. Only the demoted Cassio is absent.

Lodovico greets Othello and gives him a personal letter from the Doge. [3] While Othello reads the letter, Lodovico asks Iago where Cassio is. Iago tells him Cassio is a *persona non grata* where

[3] The Doge is the chief magistrate of Venice, not a four-footed animal.

Othello is concerned. Desdemona innocently says she is fond of Cassio and he will soon be back in Othello's good graces. Othello overhears her and moves to strike her causing Lodovico to gasp in amazement. Lodovico asks Iago if this can really be the glorious hero everyone reveres. Iago defends him by saying, "He is what he is, I'm afraid". (With a friend like Iago ...)

Cassio enters. Othello now reveals the contents of the letter which states the Doge has called Othello back to Venice and Cassio will replace Othello as governor and commander of the military of Cyprus. The contents of the letter cause different responses. Othello and Cassio say the Doge's wish is their command. Othello is ready to leave the next day. Roderigo is feeling sorry for himself because his beloved Desdemona will be leaving the island. A furious Iago says to himself that they can all die and go to hell. Othello remembers he is angry with Desdemona and throws her to the ground. Lodovico, Desdemona, and all the onlookers, except Iago, cannot understand Othello's crude and belligerent behavior.

Iago decides to take further advantage of the situation. He presses Othello to take his revenge on Desdemona that very evening. He promises to get rid of Cassio at the same time. Of course, Iago is too clever to do the dirty work himself. He knows how Roderigo feels about Desdemona, so he talks Roderigo into killing Cassio so Othello (and Desdemona) will have to stay on Cyprus. Roderigo readily agrees; he does not know his beloved Desdemona is also on Iago's hit list. All leave except Othello and Iago. As the others leave, they are accompanied again by the crowd singing, *The Lion of San Marco*. Othello is so angry at Desdemona and Cassio he doesn't hear the crowd's plaudits. His anger and frustration cause him to convulse in a faint. Iago gloats in triumph over the motionless body of Othello. He says sarcastically to no one in particular, "Here is your Lion!".

ACT FOUR

Desdemona's bedroom. By the bed is a prayer bench, and above it is an image of the Madonna. There is a table nearby where a candle is burning. It is later that evening. Emilia is helping Desdemona prepare to retire. Desdemona has a premonition of doom. She tells Emilia about her mother's maid who sadly sang a pathetic ballad, *The Willow Song* (Weeping Willow?) after her lover jilted her. Desdemona sings it now. She gives her ring to Emilia for safekeeping. She embraces Emilia and bids her farewell forever as a worried Emilia leaves. Emilia has not seen Desdemona behave like this before. Desdemona kneels before the image of the Madonna and prays a beautiful *Ave Maria* before going to bed. She lies down and goes to sleep.

Othello enters. He extinguishes the candle, leaving the room in almost total darkness. He stares down at the sleeping Desdemona, leans over, and kisses her three times. (Remember the three kisses at the end of Act One?) The third kiss awakens Desdemona. Then a fierce dialogue begins between the two; Othello is the accuser and Desdemona the defender. He demands she confess, but she cannot because she is only guilty of loving him. She disputes Othello's charge that she loves Cassio. Othello threatens her. She begs for her life, but it's to no avail. Othello's jealousy and anger get the best of him (actually we haven't seen much best in Othello). Othello strangles her in her bed (a punster might call Othello a practical choker) as Iago had cruelly suggested. As he stares down at her, a knock is heard at the door. Emilia enters and breathlessly tells Othello that Cassio has killed Roderigo. Othello has diff- iculty believing Cassio is still alive. Desdemona faintly calls out and a shocked Emilia runs to her side. Desdemona says she is dying. She says she is an innocent victim, and she did it herself. Before she can say more, she dies. Othello says she's a liar; she didn't kill herself. He said he killed her because of her unfaithfulness. He offers the word of Iago as proof. Emilia calls him a fool for believing Iago. (Wives do know their husbands rather well.) She rushes from the room screaming for help.

Lodovico, Cassio, Iago, Montano, and a number of soldiers respond to Emilia's call for help. Emilia confronts Iago regarding Desdemona's supposed unfaithfulness. They find out what the audience has known all along — that Iago had planted the handkerchief in Cassio's lodging. As if that is not enough proof, Montano tells the group the dying Roderigo confessed to him about Iago's evil schemes. Iago decides it's time to leave and flees from the room. Several of the soldiers rush out in pursuit.

Othello finally realizes he has accused and murdered an innocent woman who loved only him. In his grief and agony, he moves over to the bed, takes a dagger from his doublet, and stabs himself.[4] He falls across Desdemona's lifeless body, saying and doing what he has said and done before, *Un bacio ... un bacio ... un altro bacio* (A kiss ... a kiss ... another kiss). With those three kisses to her lifeless body, Othello dies. Only Cassio, who is now the new governor, can be happy with this tragic ending. (Although Emilia is probably very glad to get rid of Iago.)

[4] A doublet is a tight-fitting jacket, not an Othello lookalike.

FIVE YEARS LATER
(A Fabricated and Unauthorized Epilogue)

- Cassio has been governor of Cyprus since the Doge's edict. He married his mistress Bianca and they have twins: Otho and Desdi. He has banned the carrying of concealed handkerchiefs on the island. (Statistics show incidents of hank-ky-panky are down.)

- Iago was given a dishonorable discharge but escaped further punishment for his part in the death of Desdemona. However, he was arrested and found guilty of filing false and creative tax returns. He is currently serving a 15-year prison term in Levoksia.

- Emilia divorced Iago and has lived happily ever after.

- The old soldier Montano retired with full military honors. He is writing his memoirs while he fades away.

- Lodovico, the Venetian ambassador, retired from politics. He now owns a rent-a-gondola business in Venice.

- The Doge was honored with his 20th year of service earlier this year. (Every Doge has his day.)

- The Herald changed careers. He is now a troubadour and hopes to start his own band.

***

Lohengrin
By Richard Wagner
(1813-1883)
Libretto by the composer, Richard Wagner

MAIN CHARACTERS

Henry the Fowler, King of Germany	Bass
Lohengrin, a knight of the Grail	Tenor
Elsa of Brabant	Soprano
Godfrey, Elsa's brother	Soprano
Frederick of Telramund, Count of Brabant	Baritone
Ortrud, Frederick's wife	Mezzo-soprano
The King's Herald	Bass

Place: Antwerp
Time: First half of the Tenth Century
First Performance: Weimar; August 28, 1850
Original Language: German

Richard Wagner (REEKKH-art VOGG-ner to you new opera fans) is one of the very few composers who wrote both the music and text for his operas. Wagner wrote *Lohengrin* early in his career (he was in his mid-30s) and he was able to complete this fine opera in less than a year. He wrote the last act first: Evidently he couldn't wait to see how it came out. However, Wagner wasn't around when *Lohengrin* premiered in Weimar some three years later. It wasn't that he couldn't get a ticket; he couldn't even get into his home country. At the time of the opera's premiere, he was in exile in Zurich. Turns out he had participated in a revolution in Dresden shortly after completing *Lohengrin* and had to leave town and country in a hurry.

While in Zurich, Wagner wrote a letter to Franz Liszt asking and entrusting him to produce *Lohengrin*. Liszt did so at a cost of around $1,500 — a high, unprecedented cost for operas in those days.[1] Liszt was a good guy to ask and entrust.

[1] Of course the cost wasn't in dollars – it was in thalers. It cost almost 2,000 thalers. If you have any thalers, the conversion rate to dollars may be different now.

He was not only a great friend; he was the conductor at Weimar, a position of great musical power and influence. Evidently Wagner returned the favor. Wagner's second wife was Liszt's daughter, Cosima, nicknamed the "Stork." Somehow it's difficult to imagine an attractive woman with that nickname (actually, other images come to mind). *Lohengrin* became a hit almost from the very beginning. Poor Wagner. He not only missed the premiere, but because of his exile he was to wait 13 years after completing *Lohengrin* to see a performance. During those years he ironically claimed that he was the only German who had not seen *Lohengrin*.

ACT ONE

(Scene One): An open meadow on the banks of the river Scheldt near Antwerp. King Henry the Fowler is seated on a throne beneath a massive oak tree.[2] Standing beside him are the knights and counts that have traveled with him to this part of his dominion. Across from him are the knights and nobles of Brabant, representing the local leadership of this region.

The King's Herald announces the King's Court is in session. King Henry tells the assembly he has come to this part of his dominion to mobilize an army to defend his lands from a threatened invasion by the Hungarians. He calls on the listening knights of Brabant to unite and assemble their thralls. (Some of the knights probably looked at each other with the same question — what are thralls?)[3] The knights pledged their support, although some were definitely not enthralled.

With that issue out of the way, the King asked Count Frederick of Telramund why there is so much strife within Brabant. Frederick responds by accusing his ward, Elsa, of killing her brother, Godfrey. He says he was made guardian

---

[2] Some assumptions about Henry's surname – he likes to bird hunt, he's a polluter, or he's known to hit opponents in a basketball game.
[3] In case you don't know – a thrall is a person who is in servitude. You probably don't have any thralls, but you may be one. (Wonder if knights had to report thralls on their annual tribute tax?)

of Elsa and Godfrey shortly before their father, the Duke of Brabant, died. After the Duke died, Elsa and Godfrey were in the immediate line of succession to rule Brabant. The motive for murder, Frederick claims, was to clear Elsa's path to solely rule Brabant. Frederick doesn't mention the fact that Elsa would not marry him. Rejected by Elsa, Frederick married Ortrud (sounds like a good name for a bug repellent), the daughter of Radbod, Prince of Friesland. By his marriage to Ortrud and the death of the Duke, Frederick is now claiming to be the ruler of Brabant. Possibly the King is a little confused with all the names and relationships being bandied about, but he does understand Frederick is making a serious charge against Elsa. He orders Elsa be brought forward immediately for testimony and trial.

(Scene Two): Elsa, timidly and sorrowfully, comes forward. She sings a dramatic soliloquy known as *Elsa's Dream* about a dream in which a knight (one of those guys in shining armor) comes to rescue her in a time of deep distress. Because of her demeanor, it's difficult for most of the assembly to believe she's guilty of murder. Frederick says her looks and behavior are just an act. He is angered and somewhat perturbed that anyone would doubt his word and accusation. He feels his honor is at stake. He dares any in the assembly to fight him if they doubt him. None is willing to stand up to him — or, for that matter, even sit down for him.

Not having any witnesses and with he-said-she-said testimonies, the King decides the truth of the matter and the case will be decided by judicial combat. (Judicial combats stopped a lot of frivolous lawsuits in those days.) Elsa pleads for a champion and vows she will marry whoever responds to her pleas, regardless of whom the champion is. Frederick is confident and ready to take on all comers. (Obviously, Frederick has a good scouting system.) The Herald makes a call for someone to serve as Elsa's champion. No one comes forward. (Just as obvious, the assembled knights also have a good scouting system.) Elsa is asked to give it up, but she asks that the Herald's call be made again. While the Herald's second call is made, she prays the knight of her dream will come rescue her. Almost immediately, the assembly sees a man approaching in a skiff drawn by a single swan (meaning one swan, not an unmarried swan).[4] The man is Lohengrin, and although no one knows his identity, they do perceive he is a knight. (Maybe it's because the perceptive assembly sees he is wearing a silver coat of mail, has a shining helmet on his head, has a shield by his side, and is leaning on a sword.)

Elsa's Swan Song?

(Scene Three): The swan brings the skiff to shore (at the swan-stop) and Lohengrin alights. The coming of Lohengrin, the unknown knight and presumed champion, causes mixed reactions. Elsa, naturally, cries out in joy and relief. Frederick looks worried; this guy is not on any of his scouting reports. Ortrud, Frederick's wife, loses her haughty look and shows almost an unholy terror — but more toward the appearance of the swan than that of Lohengrin (more on that later). The assembly is elated, perhaps in anticipation of the upcoming

[4] He's in a skiff, a light rowboat. If he were in a quarrel, he would be in a tiff.

duel. (Everyone seems to be ignoring the strangeness of a swan-powered skiff.)

Lohengrin gives homage to the King and tells him he is there to be Elsa's champion, if she will have him. Knowing the alternative, she happily agrees to be his championee. She also consents to be his wife as she promised. (Why not? He is known to have one suit of armor, a skiff and a swan. He might even have a few thralls.) Lohengrin tells Elsa when (not if) he wins she must promise him she will never, never ever ask his name, his rank or anything about his past. Elsa promises she will not ask him those questions. For emphasis, Lohengrin repeats the conditions to Elsa and asks if she understands them. Elsa says she understands the conditions and she will not ask those questions. (Lohengrin probably can't see her crossed fingers.)

The King now demands the judicial trial begin. Both combatants ready themselves and ask God that their honor be upheld. The field of battle is marked off and the King strikes a shield three times with his sword to signify the start of the duel. The fight does not last long; Lohengrin attacks and with a mighty stroke fells Frederick. Frederick is not mortally wounded, but he lies helpless on the ground at Lohengrin's sword point. Lohengrin generously spares his life. All in the assembly are happy with the results except Frederick, Ortrud, and a few of their cronies. The assembly celebrates as they lead the triumphant Lohengrin and Elsa to the Fortress at Antwerp. The beaten Frederick and dismayed Ortrud are left behind.

ACT TWO

(Scene One): The Fortress of Antwerp. Steps leading up to a cathedral are in the foreground. At the rear is the abode of the knights. Near the front, by the steps, is the Kemenate, the dwelling of the women. It is night, shortly after the judicial combat.

Frederick and Ortrud are seated on the steps of the minster. (A minster is a large or important church — they are not sitting on a member of the church staff.) Sounds of merriment can be heard in the distance. In contrast, Frederick and Ortrud are bemoaning their fate. Frederick says nothing about being lucky to be alive. Instead, Frederick complains to Ortrud her eye-witness report of Elsa murdering Godfrey was evidently wrong. Now he has lost his name, title, and estate. Ortrud tells him not to worry. It may look like Heaven is on the un-known knight's side, but she knows how to get vengeance. She heard what the knight asked Elsa to promise. All that is necessary, she says, is to find out the knight's name and origin — if that happens, the unknown knight will lose his power. (So, it's not a haircut — hmm, that must be another story.) She says Elsa will be the means by which they discover the needed information. She will convince Elsa the knight won by sorcery — once convinced, a suspicious Elsa will then make an effort to find out the knight's secret name and origin.

(Scene Two): Elsa appears on a Kemenate balcony above the two plotting losers. Ortrud calls out to Elsa and asks for pity. Ortrud tells Elsa how sorry she is (and she'll get sorrier as the opera goes on). She hopes Elsa will forgive her for her husband's accusations. She convinces the naive Elsa it was all Frederick's fault and she is paying for the disgrace and loss of prestige from his "wild delusions." Elsa has pity on Ortrud. She promises Lohengrin will not refuse her when she asks that Frederick be forgiven and pardoned. Elsa even invites Ortrud to come to her wedding with Lohengrin in the morn-ing. Ortrud feigns happiness for Elsa and pledges her friendship. Then, as a supposed friend, Ortrud warns Elsa that Lohengrin may be unfaithful to her — he came as if by magic and his glamour is deceptive. She says if Lohengrin really has nothing to hide and if he loves her and trusts her, he will tell her his name and origin. The seed of doubt has been planted.

(Scene Three): Morning breaks over the area where Frederick and Ortrud were seated the night before. The area is deserted now. *Reveille*, heard from the castle's turret, serves as the wake-up call for the castle cadre. Gradually servitors of the castle come into the area and begin to perform their morning chores. And, it's also time for the morning news. The King's Herald comes forward to voice two decrees of the King. First, Frederick and anyone who associates with him are deemed *personae non gratae*. Second, Lohengrin is named the Guardian of Brabant. Lohengrin has evidently refused the title of Duke, but has accepted the title of Guardian. A chorus of people (the early-risers) sings their assent.

(Scene Four): The King's Herald speaks again, informing the crowd that Elsa and her champion are to be married today and they are all invited to take part in the festivities. Talk about short notice — the next thing that happens is the entry of Elsa in her wedding dress, accompanied by her bridal attendants. They move slowly toward the cathedral from the Kemenate. As she reaches the cathedral steps, Ortrud blocks her path. Ortrud now reveals her true character, acting haughty and cruel toward Elsa, and quite differently from the humble Ortrud Elsa saw and heard the night before. She taunts Elsa and says she doesn't even know the name of the man she is marrying (Nah, nah, nee, nah, nah). She tells Elsa that he will never be true to her. Elsa is bewildered by this sudden change in her supposed friend. She is greatly disturbed and uncertain what to do. A chorus announcing the King's arrival interrupts their musical chitchat.

(Scene Five): The King and Lohengrin enter as part of a stately procession. Ortrud's continued taunting of Elsa interrupts their entry. Lohengrin demands Ortrud leave and stop causing doubt in Elsa. Now, Frederick gets into the act by making a direct plea to the King. Frederick claims he has been done a grievous wrong — the judicial combat and judgement were duped by sorcery. He accuses Lohengrin of winning unfairly, a victory that was won by unholy and evil means. He insists he will be exonerated if Lohengrin will state his name and origin. Lohengrin disputes Frederick's accusations and states no one can command him nor compel him to state his name except his love, Elsa.

The King believes Lohengrin, not Frederick, trusting Lohengrin without needing further information. The knights in the procession also say they trust Lohengrin. (It's wise to be on the side of the king.) Frederick does not lose easily. As he leaves he taunts Elsa much as Ortrud has done. (Some more "nah, nah, nee, nah, nahs"?) He repeats Ortrud's lie by telling her she can never trust Lohengrin unless she knows his name and origin. Again, Lohengrin has to tell one of Elsa's tormentors to leave and stop bothering his betrothed. Finally, the tormentors step aside and the procession can move forward. The bridal pair is free to be married by the minister at the minster. Elsa, still greatly bewildered, embraces Lohengrin, but turns her head away when she sees Ortrud grinning at her fiendishly and triumphantly.

ACT THREE

(Scene One): The bridal chamber after the marriage vows. The wedding party enters in a gay and festive mood. The ladies enter first with Elsa in tow. Following closely behind are the King, Lohengrin, and the men in the wedding party. All join together singing their blessings and congratulations to the newlyweds in the well-known *Bridal Chorus* (better known to us as *Here Comes the Bride*). At the conclusion of the song, the newlyweds embrace. The King approaches the couple and gives them his personal blessing. Then, the wedding party leaves as the music of *The Bridal Chorus* continues to play in the background. (Nowadays the wedding reception is celebrated someplace other than the bridal suite — probably a change for the better.) After all the wedding guests leave, Lohengrin and Elsa are by themselves for the first time since they met.

(Scene Two): Lohengrin and Elsa express their love to each other over and over. However, the seeds of doubt planted in Elsa's mind have done their damage. She continues to do what she promised she wouldn't do. She repeatedly asks Lohengrin about his name and origin. She feels she cannot trust him and she worries he will leave her. Her pleas are interrupted when Frederick and four other assailants burst into the room with drawn swords. Lohengrin responds quickly to their ill-advised attack by killing Frederick with one massive stroke of his sword. (Frederick either had a short memory or a severe learning disability.) Seeing their leader is dead, the four assailants lay their swords down and kneel in front of Lohengrin. (Frederick's henchmen do not have a learning disability.) Lohengrin orders Frederick's corpse to be taken to a called meeting of the assembly. He says he will tell all that Elsa has asked at the assembly.

(Scene Three): The open meadow on the banks of the river Scheldt by Antwerp (the same place of judgment as in Act One). The King and his assembly are gathered together at the request of Lohengrin. The King senses some dire event has brought them together. Lohengrin, the Guardian of Brabant, arrives and is cheered by the assembly — they are ready to follow his leadership and await his word to send them into battle. The King and his assembly are destined for disappointment.

Lohengrin addresses the court in a firm but sad manner. He tells them he came to Brabant to defend the cause of virtue, not to lead them into battle nor defend their country. He was willing to be their guardian, but now he is no longer able to accept that role. He has been driven from that role, their country, and from the side of his wife because she has broken her oath to him. She has asked and almost demanded he divulge his name and origin. Now, he will reveal his name and origin to all of them. His name is Lohengrin, the son of the mighty Parsifal (aka the Percival of English literature — with that name his father had better be mighty). Parsifal and his knights are keepers of that sacred treasure, the Holy Grail. Their life and service are attached to the Holy Grail. Lohengrin's high calling and responsibilities are to protect the Holy Grail, fight the spirits of darkness and defend high causes of virtue. Now that his name and origin are known he must return from whence he came.

While he is talking, the skiff with the swan returns and docks at the swan-stop. The assemblage is hushed; Elsa is in tears and despair. Ortrud is cackling with glee that her devious plan has led to Lohengrin's departure and that everyone is so sad. She cares less that her husband is dead. To rub it in, Ortrud tells the assembly with obvious pleasure that Godfrey is not dead. She had cast a spell on him and turned him into a swan (that's what disturbed her so much when she saw the swan when Lohengrin first came — remember?).

Lohengrin is silent. He remains silent as he kneels briefly in prayer. Then he rises and loosens the chain from around the swan's neck. Immediately the swan is magically transformed into a human form — it's Godfrey! (Godfrey is listed as a soprano, but he is silent. Has he been emasculated by this re-transformation?) Godfrey's unexpected return is welcomed by all except Ortrud, who falls to the ground as if dead.

Lohengrin boards the skiff and it slowly makes its way down the river from whence it came. (There are probably some of you who won't believe this, but a white dove now powers the skiff.) Elsa realizes she has lost her true love by her lack of trust. She cries out and then seemingly dies in her brother's arms. (In some performances she dies, in some performances she faints — no matter, she's still around for applause after the final curtain.)

FIVE YEARS LATER
(A Fabricated and Unauthorized Epilogue)

– Henry the Fowler, King of Germany, negotiated a peace treaty with the Hungarians. His enemies and detractors are now calling him Henry the Chicken — behind his back, of course.

– Lohengrin traveled to other parts of the world defending high causes of virtue similar to his deeds in Brabant. During these sojourns, he was married two more times. Both marriages lasted less than one day — his wives could not take the taunting of other women and forced him to reveal his name. (Nah, nah, nee, nah, nah.)

– Elsa did not die when Lohengrin left. She recovered, but abdicated her right to rule Brabant with her brother. She had her marriage to Lohengrin annulled and hasn't remarried. Because of her experience, she doesn't date knights. (She does date days.)

– Godfrey rules Brabant. He seems to be fully recovered from his ordeal as a swan; he is now a tenor. He is happily married to an attractive woman whose most striking feature is her long neck.

– Ortrud, Frederick's wife, is serving a life sentence in the Brabant Prison for the Criminally Insane. She has lost all her magical powers. She thinks she's a plow horse.

– The King's Herald has become the public address announcer for all Brabant sporting events. According to local gossip, he and Elsa are an item.

– Duke Godfrey pardoned Frederick's four henchmen, but they are not allowed to have weapons of any type. They formed a singing quartet, the Brawnys of Brabant, which performs at banquets and weddings.

– The dove and skiff have never been seen again.

***

Die Walküre
(The Valkyries)
By Richard Wagner
(1813-1883)
Libretto by the composer, Richard Wagner
The Second of Four Music Dramas that comprise the
Ring of the Niebelung

MAIN CHARACTERS

Wotan, Ruler of the gods	*Bass-baritone*
Fricka, Wotan's wife	*Mezzo-soprano*
Siegmund, Wotan's son by a mortal woman	*Tenor*
Sieglinde, Siegmund's twin sister	*Soprano*
Hunding, Sieglinde's husband	*Bass*
Brünnhilde, a Valkyrie (the title character)	*Soprano*
Eight other Valkyries	
(Gerhilde, Ortlinde, Waltraute, Schwertleite,	*Sopranos* and
Helmwige, Siegrune, Grimgerde, Rossweisse)	*Mezzo-sopranos*

Place: Legendary Germany
Time: Mythological
First Performance: Munich; June 26, 1870
Original Language: German

Richard Wagner wrote the four operas (*Das Rheingold, Die Walküre, Siegfried,* and *Die Götterdämmerung*) comprising the *Ring* cycle over a 27-year period.[1] Plan to spend 16 hours or so if you attend all four of them. And, if you like your German mythology flavoured with a dash of Nordic mythology, you'll get 16 hours or so of that at the same time. Wagner liked the *Ring* cycle so much he built a special opera house in Bayreuth just to do justice to his work — after all, it is 16 hours and he did write the libretto as well as compose the music.

A word about the Valkyries: These are the nine daughters resulting from a lengthy affair between Wotan, the ruler of

[1] Title Translations: *The Rhinegold, The Valkyrie, Siegfried,* and *Twilight of the Gods.*

the gods, and Erda, an earth goddess. The Valkyries' sole mission is to bring heroes to Valhalla, a place where warriors who have died in battle are received by the gods. A Valkyrie whether on or off the job, is always seen in full battle armor, which includes a breastplate, a spear, and a horned Viking helmet. They get from place to place via their flying horses without any airport or weather delays. But don't hitch a ride unless you want to go to Valhalla.

ACT ONE

(Scene One): The inside of a crude dwelling built around the trunk of a massive tree (talk about a roomy tree house). The hilt of a great sword protrudes from the trunk of the tree. There is a fireplace on one side of the room. In the rear is a large entrance door. Opposite the fireplace is a door leading to an inner room. The room is furnished with only a table and a few chairs. Outside, a storm is subsiding.

A tired and exhausted Siegmund opens the outside door and enters. Seeing the room is vacant, he staggers across to the hearth and lies down. Sieglinde enters from the inner room thinking her husband, Hunding, has come home. She is surprised to see a strange man in her house. She accosts him, but he responds meekly by asking for a drink. She perceives she is not in danger, so she fills a drinking horn with water and brings it to him. He drains the horn and the water seems to restore his energy. She then gives him some mead to drink.[2] He tells her he was in a fight with an enemy, was disarmed and had to flee for his life. He thanks her for kindness and starts to leave. Sieglinde, however, encourages him to stay at least until her husband comes home. He agrees to do so. They exchange long looks and it is evident they are attracted to each other.

(Scene Two): The sound of hoof-beats announces the arrival of Hunding. (Actually, the hoof-beats are from Hunding's horse.) Sieglinde rushes to the door to greet him, no doubt

[2] Mead is not a diet drink – it is a fermented drink made of water, honey, malt and yeast.

to explain why she is alone in the house with a stranger. Hunding, armed with shield and spear, enters warily and suspiciously when he sees Siegmund there. Sieglinde explains Siegmund's presence, and her explanation seems to satisfy Hunding, so he allows Sieglinde to take his weapons and hang them in the branches of their in-house tree. Hunding calls for supper and Sieglinde prepares the meal and sets the table for them to eat. While she is doing so, Hunding, in an aside, notices how much the stranger's features favor his wife.

They begin to eat, and while they dine, Hunding asks Siegmund to tell them who he is. Siegmund tells them his story. He says he should be called Woeful because everything in his life has been sad. His peaceful life was interrupted many years ago when he and his father, Wolfe, came home from hunting and found their home burned, his mother slain, and his twin sister missing. He spent his youth wandering in the forest with his father until they were involved in a battle with their enemies. He has not seen his father since. It seems as if every situation he has been involved in has had an unpleasant ending.

Rather than sympathize or say "So what?" Hunding now asks him how he came to be in his house and why he is without weapons. Siegmund tells them he came to the aid of a maiden who was being forced to marry one she did not love. In his ensuing struggle with her tribesmen, the maiden was killed and his weapons were hewn from his hands. He had no choice. He was forced to flee for his life and thus, weaponless and exhausted, he arrived at their house. He asks them if there is any doubt why people call him Woeful the Wolfing. (By now, none of *us*, has any doubts — nor do we want any more proof.)

Well, Hunding is ready to call him something else, now that he has heard about Woeful's latest escapade. It seems Hunding's kinsmen (probably called Hundingers) were the ones Woeful fought with and the ones who are pursuing him. An enemy of Hunding's kinsmen is an enemy of Hunding. Hunding rises from the table in great anger. He tells Siegmund he is safe for the night, but to arm himself (what with? — a knife and a fork?) and prepare to die in the morning. Sieglinde steps between the two men, but there are no threatening gestures by either man. Hunding tells Sieglinde to prepare his evening draught and wait for him in their chamber. Sieglinde slowly moves to the kitchen cabinet and prepares her husband's nightcap. While doing so she attempts to direct Siegmund's attention to the hilt of the sword in the tree, but he has eyes only for her. Hunding gestures impatiently for Sieglinde to leave. He removes his weapons from the tree and follows Sieglinde to their chamber. As he leaves, he tells Sieg-mund he diest in the morning. ('Diest' must be a superlative form of 'die' — e.g., die, dier, diest — evidently diest is the most one can die.) Hunding closes the door and bolts it behind him.

(Scene Three): Left alone, Siegmund broods about his situation. (One wonders why, weaponless, he is still there.) His nickname, Woeful, seems to be well deserved. He cries out in desperation and frustration for the sword promised him by his father. The sword was to be provided if he were ever in need. He feels the need now. Siegmund does not see the hilt of a sword in the tree where Sieglinde tried to get him to look. (Blinded by love?) As the fire in the hearth gradually goes out, Siegmund thinks about the beauty of Sieglinde.

Quietly the lock of the chamber door is unfastened and Sieglinde steals silently into the room. She tells Siegmund she put a sleeping potion in her husband's nightcap so Siegmund could escape. She says she does not love Hunding but was forced to marry him. Ever since her marriage she has been waiting for one who would rescue her from her plight. She tells him the only weapon in the house other than Hunding's is a sword buried to the hilt in their tree. She explains that a one-eyed stranger came uninvited to their wedding party and thrust the sword in the tree. The stranger said the sword would belong to the warrior who could remove it. Many have tried — obviously without success. She believes Siegmund can remove it. Siegmund, although still woeful, is excited — maybe this is the sword his father promised him.

Suddenly, the outside door springs open, revealing a beautiful moonlit evening. They stop thinking about swords. They embrace. Siegmund sings his *Spring Song*, an expression of love, spring, and happiness. Sieglinde responds in kind. They are drawn to each other and they begin to realize they may be the long-separated brother and sister. They are overjoyed by this possibility. Eventually, Siegmund turns his attention back to the sword. He is sure the sword in the tree was left for him. He goes to the tree where the hilt of the sword protrudes. With a mighty effort, he pulls the sword out of the tree. He names the sword "Nothung," meaning Needful. The fact that he is able to pull the sword from the tree verifies they are brother and sister. They embrace with great joy and incestuous passion. They rush away from the house taking Nothung with them.

Wotan, ruler of all the gods and all but one goddess.

ACT TWO

(Scene One): A desolate, high, rocky passage in the mountains. There is a rocky ledge in the background from which one can see the valley below. Wotan, the ruler of the gods, is standing there with his favorite Valkyrie, Brünnhilde.[3] Both are dressed in battle array. Wotan is the missing, earthly father of the twins, Siegmund and Sieglinde. Wotan is aware of his earthly children's flight from Hunding. He expects the battle between Siegmund and Hunding to be joined nearby. He tells Brünnhilde to aid his children, her semi-siblings, by favoring Sigmund. The upcoming battle evidently excites Brünnhilde who leaps joyously from rock to rock shouting her battle cry, *"Hojotoho! Hojotoho! Heiaho! Heiaho!"* (Haven't we seen the Brünnhilde types in the audience of professional wrestling matches?) Brünnhilde stops her exultation when she sees Fricka, Mrs. Wotan, approaching. She warns her father of the approaching storm and decides she does not wish to be part of it. She shouts a few more *Hojotohos* and *Heiahos* and leaves quickly before Fricka arrives. (With the arrival of his battle-axe, Wotan's armament is complete.)

As Brünnhilde warned, Fricka is not pleased.[4] She lets Wotan have it with both barrels. She is angry that Hunding's marriage has been violated. Fricka reminds him she is the goddess of Marriage — she cannot tolerate the adultery and incest of Sieglinde and Siegmund. She says the gods should not tolerate it either. She demands the death of Siegmund. She also knows Wotan is the earthly father of the twins — and that fact proves his unfaithfulness and unworthiness as well. She takes the moral high ground in her arguments and wears down Wotan, ruler of all the gods and all but one goddess.

---

[3] Wotan has only one eye. Wagner doesn't reveal how Wotan lost one eye until the beginning of the opera *Die Götterdämmerung*, the fourth and last music drama in the *Ring* cycle. Wotan willingly sacrificed his eye in order to drink from the Well of Wisdom. Hope that bit of foreknowledge doesn't spoil anything for you.

[4] A study of word derivations might show that friction and perhaps fracas were derived from Fricka.

Wotan finally, reluctantly and sorrowfully agrees Siegmund must die. He gives his oath to that effect to Fricka, goddess of Marriage and evidently the head of her household. (Fricka obviously wears the robes in her family.) Fricka is pleased. Her mission is accomplished, she got her way, and she's ready to leave. Then, Brünnhilde's war cry is heard nearby. Brünnhilde is returning to see her father as Fricka leaves. On her way out, Fricka gloatingly tells Brünnhilde to ask her father what Siegmund's fate will be.

(Scene Two): Brünnhilde has never seen her father so distressed. She asks what gnaws at his heart. He decides to tell her, and all of us, the missing background regarding his earthly children and his ongoing conflict with his enemies. His story follows.

It all started when a dwarf named Alberich cursed Love to gain possession of the world's gold. He shaped a gold ring that Wotan, in his quest for greater riches, took from the dwarf without *as* much as a fare-thee-well. (Wotan wouldn't consider speaking to a dwarf because he doesn't make small talk.) Alberich angrily cursed the ring which then passed from Wotan into the possession of the giant Fafner. Alberich has threatened to regain the ring and if he does so, Wotan and his fellow gods will be overthrown. Wotan needs to repossess the ring but he has a pact with Fafner that does not allow him to directly do so. Wotan saw a way to circumvent the pact with Fafner. He would have his earthly son Siegmund regain the ring for him. He thought it was a good plan. Now, with his concession and agreement that Siegmund must die, Wotan's plan to regain the ring has failed. Not only has his plan to regain the ring failed, he also is losing a son he loves.

At the conclusion of Wotan's story, Brünnhilde says she will watch over Siegmund. (She probably didn't understand the complicated story about a dwarf, a giant, and a ring, but she was nice not to ask her distraught father to repeat it.) Wotan responds sharply to Brünnhilde's suggestion that she will watch over Siegmund. He bitterly tells her she is not to protect Siegmund, but to let Hunding win. Brünnhilde argues, but

Wotan tells her in no uncertain terms to obey. As they leave, they notice Siegmund and Sieglinde are approaching.

(Scene Three): Siegmund and Sieglinde enter. They are exhausted and out of breath. She is tormented by fear and guilt and pleads with Siegmund to flee without her. They realize Hunding and his kinsmen will catch them before long. They can hear the horns and hounds of Hunding and his pursuers as they draw closer. (It is rumored that in this point of the pursuit, Wagner considered using the ditty, *A Hunding we will go, A Hunding we will go, Heigh ho, the derry-o, a Hunding we will go.*) Siegmund declares he will not leave Sieglinde. He will make his stand there to fight and kill Hunding for the wrongs he has done to her. After all, he has been empowered with Nothung — he needs Nothung else. Sieglinde collapses out of exhaustion, fear, and perhaps a bad pun.

(Scene Four): Brünnhilde appears. She has good news and bad news. The good news is that Siegmund is a hero. The bad news is that she has come to take him to Valhalla — which is a place only dead heroes can go. Siegmund likes the good news, but he doesn't take the bad news very well. In fact, he refuses to accompany Brünnhilde unless he can take Sieglinde with him. Brünnhilde says taking Sieglinde is not an option. He has no choice — the gods have preordained his death. Siegmund refuses to accept his fate. He threatens to kill Sieglinde rather than be separated. Brünnhilde sees what great passion and love Siegmund has for Sieglinde. She becomes sympathetic to them and, defying her father, agrees to protect Siegmund in his upcoming fight with Hunding. She leaves as heavy black storm clouds surround and descend upon the area.

(Scene Five): Siegmund kisses the sleeping Sieglinde, then leaves to meet the oncoming Hunding. The storm grows fiercer. Thunder and lightning awaken Sieglinde. She can hear Siegmund and Hunding as they derisively greet and challenge each other. A flash of lightning reveals the two in mortal combat. Brünnhilde is seen with the two antagonists, shielding Siegmund and encouraging him to strike Hunding a mortal blow. Siegmund aims a blow with his sword, but his sword is shattered (Nothung is aptly named). Wotan had suddenly appeared and his spear is now defending Hunding. It was his spear that shattered the sword that ironically he had left for Siegmund via the tree. Hunding then kills the defenseless Siegmund. (Siegmund's death is the result of the Fricka finger of fate.) Brünnhilde, not wanting to face the wrath of her father, races to the side of Sieglinde and they flee together. Hunding, not realizing the gods protected him, arrogantly removes his spear from Siegmund's lifeless form. Wotan contemptuously strikes the unsuspecting Hunding dead. He is most sorrowful Siegmund had to die, but he is greatly angered by Brünnhilde's disobedience and sets out to track her down. The storm increases in its intensity.

ACT THREE

(Scene One): A rocky summit in the mountains. It is an open area bordered by pines on one side. This is the place where the Valkyries assemble as they travel toward Valhalla carrying the bodies of dead heroes, as is their mission. As the scene opens, the familiar and well-known *Ride of the Valkyries* is heard. Four of the Valkyries are there, awaiting the arrival of the other five sisters. As always, they are dressed in full armor. Four of the other sisters begin to arrive on their horses, each carrying a dead hero. They greet one another with their familiar cry, *Hojotoho! Hojotoho! Heiaho! Heiaho!* [5] Rossweisse tells her sisters not to tarry; they must hurry on to Valhalla. Sister Waltraute tells them to hold their horses, they must wait for sister Brünnhilde before they leave for Valhalla — after all, they recognize Brünnhilde is Wotan's favorite daughter. (Well, she used to be his favorite daughter.) Talk about a dysfunctional family!

The Valkyrie 4-H cry is heard again as someone else is seen approaching. It is Brünnhilde, but she doesn't have the requisite dead hero on her saddle. Instead, the Valkyries see

[5] It should have been mentioned earlier that *Hojotoho! Hojotoho! Heiaho! Heiaho!* is the result of translating *Hojotoho! Hojotoho! Heiaho! Heiaho!* from the original German text. Hope that's helpful.

that she has a woman with her, and a live one at that. As Brünnhilde and Sieglinde enter, the eight sisters surround them anxious to know what is happening. Sieglinde has a glazed look in her eyes (like a fashion model walking a runway). Brünnhilde is excited and animated. She tells her fellow equestrians that she is in flight from their father. She describes her act of disobedience and her desire to help Sieglinde, a single mother-to-be, in the aftermath of Siegmund's death. The other Valkyries do not wish to hear any more. They are petrified with fear of their father. They want no part of the disobedient Brünnhilde despite her pleas for help.

Sieglinde rouses herself from almost a catatonic condition. She bemoans her situation and yearns for death. Brünnhilde scolds her. She says Sieglinde is bearing Siegmund's child and that is reason enough to live. Sieglinde is startled by the news and her attitude immediately changes. Now, she wants to live — she asks for shelter and protection. The Valkyries remain fearful to help either her or Brünnhilde. Brünnhilde realizes she is placing all of them in jeopardy. She decides to stop running and to face Wotan. She tells Sieglinde to flee to a place in the East where the Valkyries say Wotan never goes. (Let's guess — would that be to his wife Fricka's place?) The place that Brünnhilde urges Sieglinde to hasten to is where the giant Fafner, in the shape of a dragon, is guarding the ring. (Sounds like a safe, secure place.) Brünnhilde gives Sieglinde the pieces of Siegmund's shattered sword. (Some of the Valkyries don't agree — they feel Nothung is too good for her.) Brünnhilde tells her to save the pieces of the sword for her son, whom she names Siegfried. The grateful Sieglinde rushes away. As she leaves, the clouds darken as Wotan's voice is heard.

(Scene Two): The Valkyries conceal Brünnhilde in their midst. An angry Wotan enters demanding that Brünnhilde come forward. The Valkyries attempt to intercede for Brünnhilde, but the angry Wotan believes they're weak-willed and do not understand that he must chastise a breech of faith. Brünnhilde comes out of their midst to say she is ready for her sentence. Brünnhilde will soon find out she is not ready for her sentence at all. Essentially she is disowned. No longer will she be a Valkyrie. No longer will she have a flying horse. No longer will she be able to associate with Wotan or the Valkyries. No longer will she be able to go to the places where the gods and goddesses go. She will be a mere mortal cast into a powerless sleep until the first mortal man awakens her. She will become the consort of that man — ever to do his bidding, ever to meet his demands. (Is Wotan talking about Brünnhilde being a housewife?) Brünnhilde sinks to the ground as if dead. Her sisters, who made a feeble attempt to lobby for a reduced sentence, recoil in horror. Wotan warns the sisters that if they try to help her, they will meet with the same fate. The Valkyries do not lobby further, nor do they wish to hear more. They cry out aloud and wail with sorrow as they rush in panic from the scene. (Valkyries hate long good-byes.) A horrific storm had come upon them during this climatic scene. The storm slowly subsides as the Valkyries leave.

(Scene Three): Brünnhilde remains prostrate at Wotan's feet. They are alone. Slowly Brünnhilde moves to a kneeling position. She asks him:

"Was it so shameful, what I have done,

That for my deed I so shamefully am scourged?"

She says she knew he loved his mortal children and she was only carrying out his original order to protect them. He said that is true but he had revoked that order when he doomed Siegmund to death — and, then she became disobedient to his wishes. They talk more and Wotan softens but will not turn a blind eye to her disobedience. It is obvious this parting is difficult for both of them. She draws out his love for her and asks that she not be consigned to just any man who finds her there in a deep sleep. She asks to be encircled with a magical fire-flame that will protect her from the weak and make her a prize only for the brave and the strong. Wotan agrees to her request.

Wotan embraces Brünnhilde one last time. He holds her tenderly, like a small child, in his arms. Brünnhilde sinks into a deep sleep and Wotan helps her lie down. He then calls on

Loge, the demigod of fire to appear. A wall of flame encircles the sleepnig Brünnhilde. Sadly he looks at her one more time, then departs.

Many critics have described the beautiful background music in this scene, known as *The Magic Fire Music*, as Wagner at his best. These critics probably prefer their Wagner motifs soft and gentle — many of us would agree.

FIVE YEARS LATER
(A Fabricated and Unauthorized Epilogue)

NOTE: The opera *Siegfried* is the authorized and actual epilogue that follows *Die Walküre*, although the events in *Siegfried* occur at least twenty years later. In between the two operas...

– Sieglinde, unfortunately, died while giving birth to Siegfried.

– Siegfried at age four is now as tall as Mime, the dwarf who is raising him. This is probably the last year Siegfried will see eye to eye with Mime.

– Wotan, ruler of all the gods and all but one goddess, hasn't conjured up any new way he can retrieve the ring. He's ready for Siegfried to grow up and for Fricka to go away.

– Fricka has not mellowed nor softened. She is frustrated because she has been unable to set up a group that would be the male equivalent of the Valkyries.

– Brünnhilde is still a sleeping beauty waiting for a fearless warrior to come through the wall of fire to awaken her. Her loud snoring probably keeps some of them away.

– The eight other Valkyries continue their task of bringing dead warriors to Valhalla. They complain (privately, of course) of having to do the work of nine. Also they would like some casual wearing apparel. (*Hojotoho! Hojotoho! Heiaho! Heiaho!*)

***

Index

About the Author and Illustrator

In his first published book, Charles Lake targeted operas as a good source of humorous material because of their interesting but improbable plots. His close friends are probably thinking, "What's a dilettante like him doing in a nice book like this?" It *is* surprising, because the book is about opera and Charles lacks musical talent despite the fact that he came from a musically talented family. His father played the violin, his mother played the organ and piano, and his only sister Dorothy plays the piano (as does her husband Bob). A few years of failed piano lessons sentenced Charles to be part of a grateful audience. However, his appreciation and enjoyment of classical music led him to operas and eventually his man on the street interpretation of the great opera classics in this book.

Charles, a native Texan, was a data processing system analyst before he retired. (The analyst work provided his writing experience, albeit in writing humorless technical documents.) He is a 1952 graduate of Texas A&M University with a Bachelor's degree in Statistics. He and his wife, Joyce, have been happily married for 48 years with four children and eight grandchildren. He and Joyce stay busy with activities related to their family and friends, support of their church's ministries, travel, and an occasional bridge tournament.

Mike Rooth is a graduate of Sheridan College's Interpretive Illustration program, the last class of the 20th century. A St. Catharines native, he now lives in Oakville, Ontario, where he works as a freelance illustrator. Over the past five years his work has appeared in a wide variety of publications, both local and international. This is his fourth Sound And Vision book.

Acknowledgements

The creation of a book has been an enjoyable journey for me. I did not travel that journey alone and I wish to express my appreciation to those who traveled with me.

In the initial stages, my good friend Bibb Underwood provided constructive criticism and induced me to submit sample chapters to a publisher. Bibb, a classmate of mine from Texas A&M University, is a freelance writer who contributes a weekly Profiles column and a less frequent *I Been Thinkin'* column to the *San Marcos Daily Record*. Later, Jim Hamner provided help with his excellent council and creativity. Jim, a golden friend of mine for over 40 years, is an accomplished and talented musician who is active as a church organist, pianist, and entertainer in the Dallas Metroplex. Then, in the final stages, my son-in-law Bob Merriman helped immensely by revising my computer environment. (Bob is gradually towing me into the 21st century.) And, along the way, my daughter Vicki provided some needed research assistance while my wife Joyce helped greatly by proofreading (and by adding a few quips of her own).

I also appreciate my friends who read a very early draft of a chapter and encouraged me (or bless them, said nothing). Thanks go to Raymond and Ann Murphy, Janet Underwood, Jo Hamner, Harold and Catherine Gant, Skip and Jean Johnson, Thurmond and Doris Munson, and Glen and Geri McClesky.

Finally, I am indebted to David Barber, the author of numerous books of musical history and humor, for his excellent suggestions and improvements to my text. I appreciate Mike Walsh for proofreading the text and Bruce Surtees for refinements made to the two Wagner chapters. A big thank-you goes to Mike Rooth who certainly has enhanced the text with his well-done illustrations. And, through it all, I am grateful to Geoff Savage of Sound And Vision for taking a chance on a previously unpublished author and for his sound guidance through the creation journey.

Front cover: Italian painting of Donizetti's *Luci di Lammermoor*. From the Civic Raccolta Stampe Bertarelli, Milan collection. Back cover: Illustration of Brünnhilde by Mike Rooth

First published in Canada by
Sound And Vision
359 Riverdale Avenue
Toronto, Canada, M4J 1A4
www.soundandvision.com

First printing, July 2004
1 3 5 7 9 - printings - 10 8 6 4 2

National Library and Archives Canada
Cataloguing in Publication

Lake, Charles E. Grabbing operas by their tales :
liberating the libretti / Charles E. Lake ;
illustrations by Mike Rooth. Includes index.

ISBN 0-920151-38-8

1. Operas—Librettos. 2. Music—Humor. I. Rooth, Mike II. Title.
ML2110.L192 2004   782.1'0268   C2004-903278-X

Typset in Book Antiqua
Printed and bound in Canada

Quotable Books

Quotable War Or Peace
Compiled & Edited by Geoff Savage
Caricatures by Mike Rooth
isbn 0-920151-57-4

Quotable Pop
Fifty Decades of Blah Blah Blah
Compiled & Edited by Phil Dellio & Scott Woods
Caricatures by Mike Rooth
isbn 0-920151-50-7

Quotable Jazz
Compiled & Edited by Marshall Bowden
Caricatures by Mike Rooth
isbn 0-920151-55-8

Quotable Opera
Compiled & Edited by Steve & Nancy Tanner
Caricatures by Umberto Tàccola
isbn 0-920151-54-X

Quotable Alice
Compiled & Edited by David W. Barber
Illustrations by Sir John Tenniel
isbn 0-920151-52-3

Quotable Sherlock
Compiled & Edited by David W. Barber
Illustrations by Sidney Paget
isbn 0-920151-53-1

Quotable Twain
Compiled & Edited by David W. Barber
isbn 0-920151-56-6

Books by David W. Barber & Dave Donald:

A Musician's Dictionary
preface by Yehudi Menuhin
isbn 0-920151-21-3

Bach, Beethoven and the Boys
Music History as It Ought to Be Taught
preface by Anthony Burgess
isbn 0-920151-10-8

When the Fat Lady Sings
Opera History as It Ought to Be Taught
preface by Maureen Forrester
foreword by Anna Russell
isbn 0-920151-34-5

If It Ain't Baroque
More Music History as It Ought to Be Taught
isbn 0-920151-15-9

Getting a Handel on Messiah
preface by Trevor Pinnock
isbn 0-920151-17-5

Tenors, Tantrums and Trills
An Opera Dictionary from Aida to Zzzz
isbn 0-920151-19-1

Tutus,Tights and Tiptoes
Ballet History as It Ought to Be Taught
preface by Karen Kain
isbn 0-920151-30-2

Better Than It Sounds
A Dictionary of Humorous Musical Quotations
isbn 0-920151-22-1
Compiled & Edited by
David W. Barber

The Music Lover's Quotation Book
isbn 0-920151-37-X
Compiled & Edited by
David W. Barber

Other Books

The Composers
A Hystery of Music
by Kevin Reeves
preface by Daniel Taylor
isbn 0-920151-29-9

1812 And All That
A Concise History of Music from
30.000 B.C to the Millennium
by Lawrence Leonard,
cartoons by Emma Bebbington
isbn 0-920151-33-7

How to Stay Awake
During Anybody's Second Movement
by David E. Walden, cartoons by Mike Duncan
preface by Charlie Farquharson
isbn 0-920151-20-5

How To Listen To Modern Music
Without Earplugs
by David E. Walden, cartoons by Mike Duncan
foreword by Bramwell Tovey
isbn 0-920151-31-0

The Thing I've Played With the Most
Professor Anthon E. Darling Discusses
His Favourite Instrument
by David E. Walden, cartoons by Mike Duncan
foreword by Mabel May Squinnge, B.O.
isbn 0-920151-35-3

Other Books, Cont

More Love Lives of the Great Composers
by Basil Howitt
isbn 0-920151-36-1

Love Lives of the Great Composers
From Gesualdo to Wagner
by Basil Howitt
isbn 0-920151-18-3

Opera Antics & Annecdotes
by Stephen Tanner
Illustrations by Umberto Tàccola
preface by David W. Barber
isbn 0-920151-32-9

I Wanna Be Sedated
Pop Music in the Seventies
by Phil Dellio & Scott Woods
Caricatures by Dave Prothero
preface by Chuck Eddy
isbn 0-920151-16-7

A Working Musician's Joke Book
by Daniel G. Theaker
Cartoons by Mike Freen
preface by David Barber
isbn 0-920151-23-X

Drone On!
The High History of Celtic Music
by Winnie Czulinski
isbn 0-920151-39-6

Note from the Publisher

Sound And Vision books may be purchased for educational or promotional use or for special sales. If you have any comments on this book or any other books we publish, or if you would like a catalogue, please write to us at.

Sound And Vision
359 Riverdale Avenue,
Toronto, Canada M4J 1A4.

We are looking for original books to publish. If you have an idea or manuscript that is in the genre of musical humour including educational themes, please contact us. Thank you for purchasing or borrowing this book.

To view our catalogue online, please visit us at:
www.soundandvision.com.

Geoff Savage
Publisher

The Publisher welcomes any information regarding errors or omissions, that we may make necessary corrections in subsequent printings.